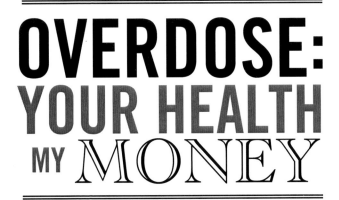

OVERDOSE:
YOUR HEALTH
MY MONEY

by **JOHN REYNOLDS, PH.D.**
and **PIERCE MCNALLY, J.D.**

Published by Charles Pinot

First Printing, 2013
10 9 8 7 6 5 4 3 2 1

Material in this book is for educational purposes only. This product is sold with the understanding that neither any of the authors nor the publisher are engaged in rendering legal, accounting, investment, or any other professional service specifically suited to one particular individual's needs who may be reading this book. Neither the publisher nor the authors assume any liability for any errors or omissions or for how this book or its contents are used or interpreted or for any consequences resulting directly or indirectly from the use of this book.

The views expressed by the individuals in this book do not necessarily reflect the views shared by the companies they are employed by (or the companies mentioned in this book). The employment status and affiliations of the authors with the companies referenced are subject to change.

Table of Contents

INTRODUCTION

Introduction

Our goal in writing this book is to contribute positively to an important ongoing national conversation. It is not designed to be a polemic or a definitive work. Our premise is that the American healthcare system, while full of dedicated professionals, is broken as a system. It is highly complex, confusing, expensive, and comparatively, underperforming. We believe our country deserves better and that it can have a better model. This book aims to discuss where we are and seeks to provide some thinking on how we got into this morass with the goal of improving our outlook. But more importantly, it is about defining the broad trends and suggesting creative solutions that would benefit from widespread public discussion and eventually adoption.

The importance of this topic to our future cannot be understated. An unhealthy country cannot be as productive as necessary in order to prosper. A healthy country cannot continue to spend an increasing—and eventually ruinous—amount of money on comparatively mediocre or sub-standard results. If this situation is not addressed aggressively and effectively to redress the flaws our healthcare system will, ironically, drown us.

We, as a country, find it difficult to discuss this topic rationally and dispassionately. It is an inherently emotional topic. It is also highly charged politically and it threatens to overwhelm us economically. There is hardly a hot button that does not get pushed repeatedly, which raises the intensity of the debate and resulting cacophony. We have all heard the rhetoric from all sides and still question whether a solution has been put forth. If an effective and affordable solution does not come out of the discussion and resulting action, we will have scuttled our own ship. If this book helps forge a national consensus in pointing to an effective and affordable healthcare future for all of us, then our aspirations for it will have been fulfilled.

Sometimes we cite sources and authorities for our assertions and sometimes we do not. When we don't, it is because we thought the underlying data was generally agreed upon, widely reported and not greatly in dispute. Again, we are not aiming to produce a definitive work, rather a conversation starter.

We do, however, make certain specific recommendations for steps to be taken that can improve our situation now. Based on trends we see, opportunities in technology, data aggregation, and increased transparency present a case for concerted action. This action can be taken by employers, individuals, regional healthcare plans, and others desiring to take advantage of elements under new federal legislation while avoiding its pitfalls. Our orientation carries a bias toward market-based solutions within a robust federal and state oversight regime. The market facing solution offers, we believe, the best chance to achieve the universal goals of better access, greater affordability, and better quality outcomes. Competition between carriers on a transparent, technology rich, and level playing field will introduce greater efficiency and cost control. Others may, and most certainly will, disagree with the wisdom of this approach. The path we are on now is clearly to expand the network of private insurance offerings to greater numbers of people. So we may as well work to make it as competitive as possible since people's healthcare needs will not wait.

Let's re-frame the context of the discussion, generate creative ideas to help people, and point ourselves towards the horizon of success.

Organization of the Book

The book has a large "cognitive load" due to the complexity of the issues surrounding the topic. In an effort to help navigate the book we have divided it into six sections:

1. Myths and Misconceptions
2. Paying the Bills
3. Re-Charting Healthcare
4. A Transformative Healthcare Model
5. Making Choices
6. CieloStar

Who Should Read This Book?

This book is primarily written for the owners, executives, and senior and middle management of any company who are struggling to understand the nature and ramifications of the revolutionary changes coming to the healthcare world. These managers likely only really understand one thing about these changes and that one thing is that they do not have a clue what's really going to happen.

They are not alone in their lack of a clear understanding of the landscape ahead. They are joined by a whole host of affected parties: from our policymakers to insurances companies, from brokers to healthcare providers and healthcare consumers.

However, the absence of an idea of what to do does not mitigate in any way the fact that they still need to make the right decisions for their companies and employees going forward.

The implications and ramifications of decisions made under the new paradigm of healthcare benefits in the corporate setting are huge. Health and other benefits are such large components of employee compensation; they can be a critical factor in the success or failure of any enterprise. Like any other significant decisions made by corporate leaders or managers, they cannot be made in a vacuum—decision makers must understand the nature of the changes and the reasons why those changes are absolutely necessary.

This book is certainly required reading for the above mentioned employer who, after having another annual meeting with his insurance broker and hearing another triumphant story about premiums only going up 12 percent, looks up to the heavens and says to anyone who will listen, "there has to be a better way!"

Through all of the complicated concepts and solutions outlined in the pages that follow, there is a reason for some optimism—solutions exist that can significantly improve the healthcare experience for the consumer and greatly improve efficiencies that ultimately go directly to the bottom line for employers. This book can help to make those solutions a reality for the participants.

AUTHOR BACKGROUNDS

John Reynolds

Dr. John Reynolds is President and Chief Executive Officer of CieloStar. His first exposure to the healthcare industry was while he was studying for his undergraduate degree. He worked as a ward clerk in a pediatric intensive care ward, which provided a great front-row seat to the industry's inefficiency and the lack of connectivity in data.

Reynolds was named President & CEO of CieloStar in August 2012 after leading the successful sale of the FIS Healthcare Division to Lightyear Capital that same month. In his previous role as President of FIS Healthcare, Government and Biller Solutions, Reynolds was responsible for achieving a market leadership position in all business lines. He drove all aspects of the businesses including full P&L, operations, technology, sales, marketing and relationship management. Reynolds' divisions incorporated several companies acquired by FIS, as well as other internally developed products and services. Prior to joining FIS, Reynolds was senior vice president and business director for Institutional Trust & Custody, Benefits Consulting, and Health Benefits Services at Wells Fargo & Co.

Reynolds has over 28 years of banking, healthcare, benefit consulting, and payment technology experience. Previously he managed Wells Fargo & Co.'s Global Trust & Custody business and additionally was responsible for Bryan, Pendleton, Swats & McAllister, LLC, an employee benefits consulting business with a national client base. He also managed sales and customer service within the Global Cash Management department of Mellon Bank Corporation in Pittsburgh, Pennsylvania.

Reynolds holds a bachelor's degree in Economics, Aeronautical Science, and Speech Communications from the University of Minnesota. He holds a Master's degree in Management and Administration from Metropolitan State University in St. Paul, Minnesota. Additionally, Reynolds earned his Ph.D. in Organization and Management from Capella University in Minneapolis, Minnesota. Reynolds is a certified flight instructor and has been an adjunct instructor of Aeronautical Science at the University of Minnesota. He has been a frequent speaker at national healthcare and financial services conferences and has published numerous articles on consumer directed healthcare, B2B healthcare payment technology, accountable care organizations (ACO's), treasury management, electronic commerce, customer loyalty, and related topics.

Pierce McNally

Pierce McNally is the Chief Strategy Officer and General Counsel of CieloStar. McNally has built a specialty over the years working with emerging companies beyond the startup phase to create the necessary business processes and procedures to deal with high growth curves and to extend successful operations beyond the initial first blush of success.

McNally graduated in 1978 from the University of Wisconsin Law School, J.D., Order of the Coif, with an undergraduate degree in history from Stanford University.

Prior to joining CieloStar, McNally was a senior attorney at Gray Plant Mooty in Minneapolis practicing in the areas of business law, corporate governance, and entrepreneurial services.

McNally has worked with start-up and early-stage companies with which he would also develop an advisory or management relationship. His work would help emerging growth companies successfully attain the next level of development. He has been affiliated with numerous companies in this way including those in the fields of industrial technology, manufacturing, business services, broadcasting, and product distribution. He has written and lectured on numerous topics pertaining to corporate governance issues including the Sarbanes-Oxley Act.

In 1983, McNally was elected to the Board of Directors of his family company, Midwest Communications, Inc., which owned numerous broadcast properties including WCCO-TV, WCCO-AM, and WLTE in the Twin Cities. In 1989, he was subsequently elected as an officer of the company and he served in both capacities until the company merged with CBS, Inc. in 1992.

He currently serves on the board of directors of numerous corporations and non-profit entities located in the Midwest and elsewhere.

SECTION I
MYTHS AND MISCONCEPTIONS

While most of us in this country don't spend a lot of time thinking about healthcare—generally we just assume it's there like our police and fire protection—when we do start to think about it or talk about it with our family or friends, a lot of things just don't make sense. Why does everything cost so much? Why does it take so long and involve so much hassle to do anything? We worry about the high cost of health insurance and complain about paying a $20 co-pay to visit a doctor.

Now if we were thinking about it logically, instead of complaining about that co-pay, we would be wondering how could that $20 co-pay possibly cover the cost of that medical professional's time? Again, logically thinking, it can't. If all that that doctor received for the 20 minutes he spent with you was $20, he would not be in business for long.

So where is the rest of the money coming from for that doctor's time? Most people who have an opinion on the subject would probably reply that it comes from his or her employer, or from the insurance company. So where does that employer or the insurance company get the money?

This is where the discussion ends, our eyes glaze over, or someone usually changes the subject.

The fact is many of us have some serious misconceptions about healthcare in this country and have become believers in some myths that upon even casual examination really don't hold water. We don't think deeply or talk in depth about it because it is a subject that can produce significant anxiety. It can be uncomfortable to think that because of high costs and budget cuts, the fire department might not show up in time to save my house. It's the same kind of discomfort and anxiety that keeps us from applying what may be a really reliable "smell test" to the subject of healthcare in this country.

This is very emotional stuff—not only for individuals but also for employers. It's equal or next to our financial security and well-being as far as our big picture priorities stand, and it is in exactly the same position for most employers. For employers there is the inevitable cost of employee healthcare, but also the sense of well-being and security it provides the employee, a less tangible yet very real benefit.

It's time for both employers and individuals to set aside the misconceptions and look at the myths at face value. That's what we will try to accomplish in this section.

The Political Conversation Has Failed Us

There are two assumptions in this country that have in many ways shaped and directed our national conversation around healthcare policy. This critical conversation among citizens and politicians alike, has in essence, been diverted in a direction that misleads people and obscures what should be the real topic of that national conversation.

The first of those assumptions is that it is normal—even expected—that employers provide healthcare benefits to their employees. The second assumption is that "someone else" pays for healthcare in this country and that there is somewhere an unlimited pool of money to pay for our rising healthcare costs.

These assumptions are at the core of decades of legislation and policy discussion and it is the result of these assumptions that has become the basis of the broken healthcare system that we are faced with today.

Our healthcare system as we know it today was established in the 1940s, during World War II. At the time, because of the war, it was impossible for employers to raise wages so offering health benefits was a way that employers could distinguish themselves and attract the best employees. That set a precedent that picked up speed, momentum, and so much critical mass that it became the standard way things were done. This precedent led to a number of consequences, one of which is that the political conversation in this country around healthcare has not really dealt with the true nature of how healthcare should work in a country such as ours.

In order to fix a broken healthcare system—or devise one in the first place—the policy making conversation must start with consensus among the parties as to the basic assumptions and parameters that will apply equally to everyone and form the basis of a system that is as fair and equitable as humanly possible.

> In order to fix a broken healthcare system—or devise one in the first place—the policy making conversation must start with consensus among the parties as to the basic assumptions and parameters that will apply equally to everyone and form the basis of a system that is as fair and equitable as humanly possible.

The most basic of those assumptions and parameters, and the one that should have formed the basis of our healthcare system all those decades ago is this: no matter what kind of a system is envisioned, at the end of the day we all pay for healthcare in this country. The young are going to pay for the old, the healthy are going to pay for the sick, and by extension, the wealthy are, in some measure, going to pay for the poor. Go anywhere in the world where governments have had long histories of dealing with this precise issue and they will all agree that this is the immutable truth about healthcare. The sooner those countries came to a consensus on that issue, the faster problems could be solved and a coherent system established.

If a nation has not built that kind of political consensus, it's almost impossible to set up a workable system. People and politicians must accept the inherent inequity of those parameters and move on before a real conversation about creating as fair and equitable a system as is possible given the imbalance of the original parameters.

In this country our political conversation around healthcare has never actually focused on these self-evident truths, and until we do—until we accept that despite the fact that it is inequitable, that the young pay for the old, the healthy pay for the sick, and the wealthy in some measure pay for the poor—it is going to be impossible to figure out how to devise a system that addresses the major issues of accessibility, affordability, and quality of outcome.

Will we ever get there? Can we reach that kind of national consensus? Can we get beyond the political partisanship, the divisive cries of "socialized medicine," "prioritized Social Security," "death panels," and other manufactured taboos?

It's unfortunate that we can't simply have a frank conversation about national healthcare without the partisan bickering and posturing. We would find that the challenges we face are no different than those faced by Germany, England or Canada. But it's a matter of actually having that conversation. It is the only way we really figure out what the driving assumptions and parameters are around our healthcare and establish a fair, equitable system within those constraints so we can move forward and start improving our system, reduce costs, and increase accessibility.

Other than the public debt and our national deficits, dealing with our healthcare system is clearly the single largest fiscal challenge that we face. Healthcare amounts to at least $2.5 trillion out of an approximate $14 trillion a year economy. This is a huge slice of the U.S. economy and it is growing at double-digit rates. If those expenditures continue to expand at the current rate it will eat up the entire economic output of this country. The sheer economic force of it will require that the conversation around how to do it better keeps going.

International Comparison of Spending on Health, 1980–2010

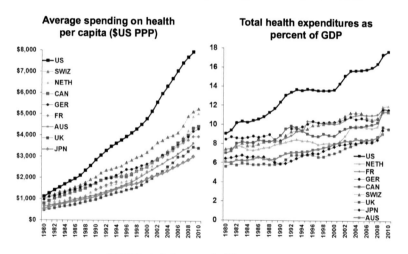

Notes: PPP = purchasing power parity; GDP = gross domestic product.
Source: Commonwealth Fund, based on OECD Health Data 2012.

The United States is arguably the wealthiest country in the industrialized world. We spend more on healthcare than any other country. How can our infant mortality rates be increasing? How can our life expectancy not be as good as other countries? The relevant statistics do not paint an optimistic story. We spend more than anyone else and our outcomes are not keeping pace, in fact, they are getting worse. The following graphs and charts help to illustrate some of the areas of deep concern.

Health spending as a share of U.S. gross domestic product (GDP) has climbed steadily over the past half-century. Today it constitutes 18 percent of GDP, up from 14 percent in 2000 and 5 percent in 1960, and we are well on our way to 21 percent by 2023, based on current projections. This increased dedication of economic resources to the health sector, however, is not yielding commensurate value in terms of improving population health or patients' experiences with care.

Premiums Rising Faster Than Inflation and Wages

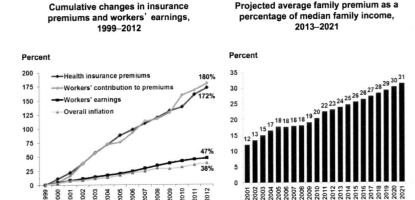

Sources: (left) Kaiser Family Foundation/Health Research and Educational Trust, *Employer Health Benefits Annual Surveys, 1999–2012*; (right) authors' estimates based on CPS ASEC 2001–12, Kaiser/HRET 2001–12, CMS OACT 2012–21.

On average, the U.S. spends twice as much on healthcare per capita, and 50 percent more as a share of GDP as other industrialized nations do. Yet we fail to reap the benefits of longer lives, lower infant mortality, universal access, and quality of care realized by many other high-income countries. There is broad evidence, as well, that much of that excess spending is wasteful. Stabilizing health spending and targeting it in ways that ensure access to care and improve health outcomes would free up billions of dollars annually for critically needed economic and social investments—both public and private—as well as higher wages for workers.

> On average, the U.S. spends twice as much on healthcare per capita, and 50 percent more as a share of GDP, as other industrialized nations do. And yet we fail to reap the benefits of longer lives, lower infant mortality, universal access, and quality of care realized by many other high-income countries.

A comparison of inflation in insurance premiums, workers contribution to premiums, workers' earnings, and overall inflation reveals another unsustainable trend.

The average annual growth rate for health insurance premiums has been steadily rising over the past 13 years. During this period public and private efforts to rein in accelerating costs have included wage and price controls, voluntary hospital cost containment, managed care, and the threat of health reform. In some cases these efforts have triggered sharp declines in spending growth, but these periods of decline have proven temporary and have been followed by rapid growth in costs.

How can we spend so much and get so little return on those expenditures? One of the reasons is that our healthcare system is highly inefficient. For example, there's too much manual intervention generating too much paper, both of which drive up costs. Every time there's a piece of paper that needs to be touched by a human, the cost of that healthcare skyrockets.

How wasteful is the system? Data provided by The Institute of Medicine indicate that at least 30 percent of every dollar spent is going to waste through truly unnecessary administrative overhead as well as other factors. Viewed as 30 percent of the $2.5 trillion spent on healthcare really gives proper perspective on just how wasteful our system is— almost $1 trillion worth!

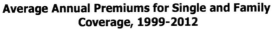

Average Annual Premiums for Single and Family Coverage, 1999-2012

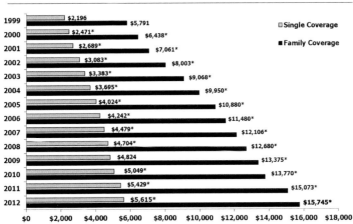

* Estimate is statistically different from estimate for the previous year shown (p<.05).

Source: Kaiser/HRET Survey of Employer-Sponsored Health Benefits, 1999-2012.

The level of waste and more importantly, inefficiency, can be subtle and insidious. Take for example an icon of healthcare in this country, the Mayo Clinic in Minnesota. When one thinks of the Mayo Clinic, one expects nothing but the best. There's no question that it is one of the best healthcare providers in the country, if not the world. They even have their own in-house mobile and web-based applications for the purpose of tracking lab results, doctor's notes, etc. when one is a patient there. But all of the considerable resources and consumer-directed features stop at the clinic's doors. None of the patient records that are part of their systems are connected to the outside world. A patient's experience at the Mayo Clinic doesn't get connected to his medical records elsewhere.

As the graphic below depicts, the United States is making progress in the adoption of electronic medical records. However, it should be noted that unlike other developed countries that already have high adoption rates, their citizens' medical records are more easily shared from and among providers. So while the U.S. is showing increased penetration, it has still not solved the issue of "sharing" information from provider to provider. In the United States, unless all of your care occurs within one health system, there is no central view of health history.

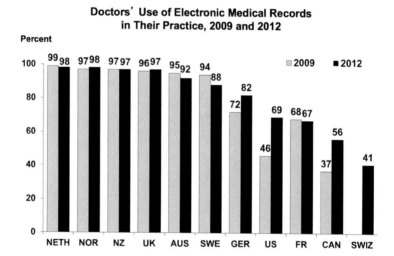

Doctors' Use of Electronic Medical Records in Their Practice, 2009 and 2012

Source: 2009 and 2012 Commonwealth Fund International Health Policy Survey of Primary Care Physicians.

Not only is this lack of connectivity annoying and inconvenient, it's potentially dangerous as well as obviously inefficient. If that Mayo Clinic patient goes to another doctor where those records are relevant, someone has to either physically obtain paper copies of those records or make a special request to receive electronic records before they are of any use. In other words, the exchange of data is anything but immediate and when needed in an emergency, may not be available in time to avoid misdiagnosis or mistakes.

Back to myths, misconceptions, and assumptions—who pays for all of this healthcare?

Ask someone in Germany how healthcare is paid for in his country and he might say that the German healthcare system operates on the basic principle that it's a shared risk system between the young and old, the healthy and the sick, and the public and the private sectors. Ask an American the same question and he might say that the insurance companies pay. Our national conversation around healthcare has always implied that "somebody else" pays for healthcare. The insurance companies. Employers. The truth that has not been embraced by our politicians and citizens is that we all pay for healthcare – and we pay dearly for it.

Take a step back and think about it. Insurance was never meant to pay for routine visits to a doctor. Auto insurance doesn't pay for an oil change or a new battery. Health insurance, if it's truly insurance and not indemnity, insures someone against catastrophic events, just the way car insurance insures against collision or theft or some other catastrophic event. Car insurance doesn't pay for new tires; that's wear and tear and comes out of the owner's pocket. If auto insurance was designed to cover that kind of expense, premiums would have to be considerably more costly.

Going forward, Americans can't expect insurance companies to pay for routine doctor visits without also expecting to pay very large sums of money in premiums. Many other countries have already had this conversation and accepted this reality a long time ago. In America, we have just begun our conversation.

Infant Mortality and Life Expectancy

Despite the fact that as a country we spend more on healthcare than any other industrialized nation as a percentage of our gross domestic product, we are not realizing the benefits of that spending. The United States has the highest age standardized death rate for men and women when compared to France, Germany, and the United Kingdom.

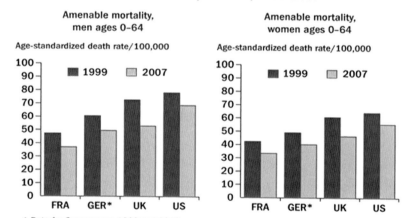

U.S. Men and Women Under Age 65 Have Higher Rates of Potentially Preventable Deaths
Slowest Rate of Improvement, 1999–2007

Amenable mortality, men ages 0–64

Amenable mortality, women ages 0–64

Age-standardized death rate/100,000

Age-standardized death rate/100,000

* Data for Germany are 1999 and 2006.
Source: Adapted from E. Nolte and C. M. McKee, "In Amenable Mortality—Deaths Avoidable Through Health Care—Progress in the US Lags That of Three European Countries," *Health Affairs*, published online Aug. 29, 2012.

To add additional support to that statement, here are two statistics from CIA.gov:

Life expectancy rates, which are measures of overall quality of life in a country, are highest in select countries in Asia and Europe. Chad holds the lowest ranking with an average life expectancy of 48.69 years. The United States ranks 51st out of 220 countries with an average life expectancy of 78.49 years (2012 Estimate). The highest life expectancy rate can be found in Monaco at 89.68 years.

Afghanistan tops the infant mortality rate with 121.63 deaths per 1,000 live births. At 1.80, Monaco has the lowest rate, which is often used as an indicator of overall health conditions in a country. The United States has 6.0 deaths per 1000 live births and ranks 173 out of 220 countries.

The data clearly shows that in this country, counter to what you would expect, key indicators of the overall health of our citizens are in decline despite how much is spent annually on care. Two indicators in particular—infant mortality and overall life expectancy—are trending in the wrong direction. Our infant mortality rates are increasing and our overall life expectancy is going down.

The trend lines in these two indicators show just how disconnected the amount of money spent in our healthcare system is from the quality of our healthcare and the outcomes. With healthcare expenditures increasing, we would expect such indicators to be improving. Turning those trends around is one of the bigger challenges we can only accomplish by changing the rules about our healthcare system.

The long-term implications of these trends and the sheer amount of money we spend in this country on healthcare—both per capita and as a percentage of our gross domestic product—are sobering, especially when looked at in relation to other industrialized nations.

Our spending is nearly double that of other industrialized nations. We spend nearly 18 percent of our gross domestic product on healthcare expenses. Our industrialized "competitors" are in the 7-10 percent range. And by competitors, we mean those countries we not only compete with in the marketplace with our products and services, but these are also the same countries we compete with to attract companies to locate their plants and offices with us.

From the standpoint of an international company looking to open facilities in the United States, the healthcare cost differential is significant. That company would be required to spend nearly twice as much on a non-productive input without the same increase in quality of result. That's money taken directly away from plant, equipment, technology, and, ultimately, labor.

> Our spending is nearly double that of other industrialized nations. We spend nearly 18 percent of our gross domestic product on healthcare expenses.

The Problem of the Uninsured

As stated previously, the primary vehicle for providing healthcare for people in this country is through health insurance—whether it's obtained through one's employer or purchased on an individual or group basis outside of a person's occupation.

If we accept that private health insurance is the fundamental means for providing healthcare (at least for the time being), then the viability and overall expense apportionment associated with that system depends on the number of participants in the "pool" of insured persons.

Uninsured consumers of healthcare can (and have) become a serious problem. Estimates place the current number of people in this country who do not have health insurance at approximately 49 million. And while there is much disagreement as to how to deal with the issues surrounding our healthcare system, all agree that these 49 million people are a significant cause in escalating the problems and costs associated with our system.

One of the key political discussion points in the years leading to the adoption of the Affordable Care Act in 2010 was the issue of the uninsured and how to bring them into the system. Bringing those uninsured into the healthcare system allows us to improve access, affordability, and hopefully, outcomes.

Those discussions not only dealt with the issue of how to insure the uninsured, but also went to even more fundamental issues of how should a re-vamped healthcare system be set up in the first place.

The political conversations were wide-ranging. On one hand were those advocating for a single-payer system—essentially make the government the "payer" and eliminate the private insurance companies. With the government as the payer, there would be universal coverage and the issue of uninsured would not exist.

The single-payer model with the government organizing, managing, and paying for care is, to say the least, controversial, even though one such system is already in place in this country at the federal level: Medicare. For all of its critics, Medicare as a single-payer system does work and many have argued that at least part of the solution to our systemic healthcare problems would be to expand the scope and reach of Medicare.

The whole concept of a government-run single payer system has never garnered overwhelming support amongst policy makers, in large part because of skepticism over mixing government and "socialized medicine." The healthcare system in England is frequently held up as an example of why a government-run single payer system does not work. Are our doctors going to work for the government, and does that system work well? The political support is just not yet there to create another government administrative system on the level of the Social Security Administration.

It's an idea that seems to appeal on a consistent basis to about one-quarter to one-third of the members of Congress—not enough to put forth an initiative susceptible of enactment.

At the other end of the political discussion surrounding the basic structure of our healthcare system is what is known as a "voucher system." In a voucher system the payer (presumably the government) would provide individuals with a voucher worth a certain amount of money and then individuals would use that "currency" to purchase the services that they need. These vouchers could be put towards a plan from a private healthcare provider, or they could be used to purchase the services of an individual healthcare professional. The individual would have the voucher and would bargain with the provider for whatever benefit he or she desired.

Those are the two extremes—single payer and voucher systems—and sitting right in the middle between them is the extensive private insurance system that we have today. It is nationwide, it is well developed, and it already supplies most of the healthcare benefits that people currently have. Will the addition of millions of uninsured to the existing private insurance model get us to these laudable goals?

As policymakers, we tend not to embrace extremes. Thus, when presented with an opportunity to re-invent our broken healthcare system, our politicians did what they usually do, they moved to the middle. With the Affordable Care Act, they in many ways settled for a plan that aims for greater accessibility to care, greater affordability of care, and greater quality of outcomes. The mechanism that they chose to begin to achieve those goals was to shoehorn the uninsured into the existing insurance system.

The Unlimited Pool of Money for Healthcare

As we continue to discuss the myths and misconceptions surrounding our healthcare system, one of the biggest ones is that there is an unlimited amount of money in this country for healthcare.

This myth is closely tied to the perception, held by many, that since they aren't paying for healthcare (they only pay premiums to the insurance company), the insurance companies must be paying for all of it. That extends to the belief or assumption that there must be this unlimited pool of money somewhere that the insurance companies use to pay for healthcare costs.

This fallacy of unlimited money for healthcare becomes an acute issue as we get older. Even if we do agree that in reality we all pay for healthcare, and that the way the system will in fact work is the young pay for the old and the healthy pay for the sick, at what point in time do we say enough is enough? Is there a point where we decide as a society that we can't pay any additional for someone's care? Here in this country we tend to make that kind of decision based on the dollar amount involved. In Canada, for example, that decision is illuminated as a function of time. In the Canadian national healthcare system, if a patient is certified as a candidate for a kidney transplant that patient is added to a waiting list. He might be number 92 on that list and can expect to get that transplant in a year or more. The doctor knows that the patient won't likely last six months. And in that way, the Canadian system exerts some control over its cost and resource management. To us, that may sound like medical triage, but is it a valid means to an end?

> This fallacy of unlimited money for healthcare becomes an acute issue as we get older.

Spending too much on someone's particular healthcare comes up most often in end of life situations. Data shows that for most of us, 75 percent of the total dollars expended for our healthcare will be spent in the last six months of our lives. The "try everything at all costs" mentality sounds noble but is it realistic? How long should someone stay connected to life support before the decision is made that enough is enough? Obviously, these are emotionally charged, extremely difficult choices and decisions, and even harder to turn into national policy.

Three-quarters of healthcare monies are generally expended in the last six months of an individual's life. Is that something that we can sustain? Is that something that we should sustain? The cynical political pundit might opine that we could solve all of the difficulties surrounding healthcare in this country if everyone—or just those 70 years or older—simply died six months earlier. Interestingly, when you conduct polls on end of life care, the vast majority of those polled do not want his or her life prolonged unnecessarily—they don't want to be "plugged into the wall." But that's exactly what happens to them when they are admitted to a hospital, especially when they have no living will that would specify their wishes for end of life. With no living will, the medical establishment has no choice but to prolong for as long as they can, consistent with the desires of the family, and there's always one family member who wants to try everything and wait forever for a result that in most cases is not going to happen.

> Three-quarters of healthcare monies are generally expended in the last six months of an individual's life.

One thought is that perhaps hospitals should not admit people for serious care without a living will. Or perhaps we are in need of more of the Canadian "waiting list" approach.

The reality is of course that there is no unlimited pool of healthcare funds. It is a fantasy. We all pay for healthcare and it is real money, not some imagined, unlimited pot of gold at the end of a rainbow.

History has shown us how the evolving healthcare system will likely play out. Extravagant healthcare funding beginning in the mid 1960's led to decades of unrestrained spending, followed by unsuccessful attempts to contain costs. In the 1990's managed care introduced business concepts that were otherwise foreign to the world of healthcare. The result was a much needed taming of expenditures, but at the price of denials, delays, and inconveniences that sometimes were medically, personally, politically, and even economically counterproductive. Although healthcare clearly needed business discipline, many of the tools of managed care came from people who had considerable experience with business, such as insurance, but little experience with the clinical nuances of healthcare.

A key development has been the erosion of the relationship between the provider and the patient. The healthcare industry in the last decade has very cleverly begun to change the vocabulary to the point that patients are now clients and not even consumers. Patients used to be people who needed the help or assistance of the provider or doctor to resolve a health issue, but now patients are clients of the provider and clients of the insurer/payer.

The ACA puts patients and providers back in the center of the process and leaves the payer in a diminished role. The traditional triad of players in the healthcare equation (Payer, Provider, and Patient – the three P's) has had an emphasis on the payer at the expense of both the patient and the provider and has largely gotten us into our current mess. The patient has become transparent in our current healthcare system. Why else have patients turned away from traditional medicine to alternatives that really see them? The patient needs to once again be seen as a person, not a financial incentive, not a resource for a product, but a real person with a problem that needs some help. The Affordable Care Act and Accountable Care Organizations, about which we talk in detail later, will make the payer transparent. The provider, whether a hospital, doctor, or urgent care center has also lost integrity in the current healthcare system. The provider is at the mercy of the payer; the provider no longer has a real relationship with the patient or the patient with the provider. In our current healthcare system it is the payer that has the bull by the horns. This bull, otherwise known as healthcare, pun intended, is controlled at the wrong end.

The Doctor Will Make Me Well

For decades in this country we've had a "drive it until it drops" mentality. We do fix things when they break, but we frequently allow them to break first. Whether it's that noise your car has been making that you know isn't right or that oil change that you should have done months ago or that blasted "Check Engine" light that we try to tell ourselves is really just a clever device invented by auto manufacturers to get us into the shop so that they can charge us for some unnecessary repair. We more likely than not tend to put off our preventative maintenance until whatever the problem is becomes acute.

It's no different when it comes to our health.

When we feel sick or something hurts, many of us typically ignore it as long as we possibly can. The last thing we want to do is take time off from work to go to the doctor. We alternate back and forth between denial—thinking that whatever it is will just go away if we ignore it—and fear that there might really be something wrong. So we do nothing. We wait until whatever it is becomes more than we can ignore.

> When we feel sick or something hurts, many of us typically ignore it as long as we possibly can. The last thing we want to do is take time off from work to go to the doctor.

We are stuck in being reactive about our health (as we are with our cars) as opposed to being proactive—or preventative.

The consequences of treating our healthcare as something to react to are not difficult to imagine. Just as the cost of rebuilding your car's engine is a lot more expensive than the periodic oil changes that would have prevented your engine from seizing up because of poor lubrication, the cost for providing "fix it" care for our health is far more expensive—individually and to the healthcare system—than preventative healthcare.

We are clearly seeing statistics and evidence that as part of our retooling of our healthcare system we must also re-train the population to take responsibility for its own wellness. Progress will only be made on such major health issues like cardiovascular heatlh and Type 2 diabetes with a significant commitment to preventative measures on the part of individuals.

The belief system must change from "the doctor will cure me" to "I am responsible for staying healthy."

We all need to take steps in our daily life that will favorably affect our well-being. One of the emphases in the Affordable Care Act is to give individuals incentives to change their behavior in this area. The only way we can make significant progress on managing and controlling the spiraling cost of healthcare is to get away from the "fix it" mentality and into a mode of "how can I live a healthier lifestyle?" Avoiding these conditions in the first place is critical because by the time it gets to the treatment stage, it becomes difficult, it becomes expensive, and it becomes burdensome for everyone in society at that point.

So remember to change your oil regularly.

SECTION II
PAYING THE BILLS

Health Insurance and Free Healthcare

There are two types of healthcare payers: government and non-government (private sector).

The government pays for healthcare through Medicare, Medicaid, and many other programs.

All types of insurance operate on the principle of shared risk. You pay premiums to an insurance company, and the company uses your premium to pay claims. When you purchase insurance, you hope never to use it. Only when the unexpected happens – an accident, storm damage, theft, or vandalism – do you file a claim. You would not expect your insurance company to pay for a fresh coat of paint on your home for sake of maintenance. Until the mid 1960's, Americans looked at their health insurance in the same way: they expected to use it only to help pay the costs of unexpected catastrophic illness or injury, not preventive care. That is why it is called catastrophic or major medical insurance.

Up until the mid 1960's, Americans paid for as much as 47 percent of their own healthcare out of their own pockets (National Health Expenditures by Type of Service & Source of Funds: Calendar Years 1960 – 2004, Centers for Medicaid and Medicare, U.S. Government). If they owned insurance it only covered major expenses that protected them from unforeseen catastrophic medical and hospital bills. People paid a fee each time they used a doctor or hospital – called a fee for service. Most people who owned health insurance expected that they might need it a handful of times during their lifetime – hopefully, never.

During the early 1960's, about six percent of U.S. residents were older than 64 and only half of those owned health insurance. Congress used that 50 percent uninsured rate as the reason to create a new centralized payment system for the healthcare needs of seniors. In 1965, Congress created Medicare to provide hospital and doctor services to seniors aged 65 and older.

Also in 1965, Congress created Medicaid, a taxpayer-paid insurance program for low-income, disabled, and aged Americans. Before this doctors often provided free care to low-income persons, and they sent them to the county hospital for severe illness or injury. Scores of charities, often faith based, provided medical care for indigents and low-income people.

> In 1965, congress created Medicare to provide hospital and doctor services to seniors aged 65 and older and Medicaid, a taxpayer-paid insurance program for low-income, disabled, and aged Americans. As a result, for the first time in United States history some Americans discovered that they were entitled to nearly free coverage for a wide range of healthcare services.

As a result of Medicare and Medicaid, for the first time in United States history some Americans discovered that they were entitled to nearly free coverage for a wide range of healthcare services. These benefits, however, exceeded those available to the vast majority of 1965 U.S. workers whose insurance only covered catastrophic illness or disease. U.S. seniors and low-income residents could now sign up for a fantastic, and nearly free, healthcare entitlement. Government now paid for most of their healthcare and patients had no clue about its costs and they didn't much care since someone else paid the bills.

Now that they were entitled to nearly free healthcare, Medicare and Medicaid patients increased their utilization of medical services – they demanded care more often. In 1965 the government spent $10.6 billion on healthcare; but that ballooned to $28.3 billion by 1970, increasing at a rate nearly twice as fast as privately paid healthcare. (No. 114. National Health Expenditures-summary. 1960 – 2002, and projections, 2003-2013, Abstract of the United States, Bureau of the Census). Healthcare spending worried the lawmakers who created the programs. Acting in the manner of politicians, to solve this funding problem Congress decided to pass more laws.

Current System: Unavoidable Inefficiency

Our healthcare system in this country as it is currently structured has almost no option other than to be horribly inefficient. It is designed with so many unnecessary layers and intermediaries, so much paper that must be manually shuffled. It seems to be a system that values complexity, inconsistent rules, delays, and above all, chaos.

Our healthcare system in this country as it is currently structured has almost no option other than to be horribly inefficient. It is designed with so many unnecessary layers and intermediaries, so much paper that must be manually shuffled. It seems to be a system that values complexity, inconsistent rules, delays, and above all, chaos.

To be fair, we live in a very large, complex country with a large and very diverse population. One would expect that in such a huge and complex marketplace things could be extremely complicated; but one would also expect there to be a trendline, an evolution, or at least a desire to improve efficiency.

That kind of movement is simply not happening in the healthcare industry. If anything, the opposite is occurring and complexity and inefficiency are on the increase. Why is this counter-intuitive and counter-productive market behavior occurring? Is it simply the overly complex market and diverse population making efficiency impossible? Here are a few reasons:

1. <u>Too Many Middlemen</u>: The design of our current healthcare system is premised on inserting as many "middlemen" (for the most part, insurance companies) in between the consumer and the professional providing the healthcare. Any solution toward efficiency needs to disintermediate this relationship and allow the physician and patient to have unfettered dialogue. This continued disconnect between consumers of healthcare and those who provide healthcare services is perhaps the biggest cause of inefficiency in our system.

2. <u>Have Technology, Just Not Using It</u>: All of the technology that is needed to make our healthcare systems far more efficient exists and has been proven. In fact, the very same technology that the healthcare industry needs to transition to already powers the extremely efficient and competitive online travel and banking industries. So if all of this technology exists to go a long way toward eliminating the 30 percent waste factor in healthcare expenditures in this country—a percentage that equates to just under $1 trillion dollars annually in waste alone—why isn't it in use by the entire

industry? The technology simply has not been deployed across the healthcare industry down to the individual healthcare provider level. If the healthcare industry would deploy the existing database and payment processing technologies already in use in similar application environments, like the banking and financial services industries, there would be tremendous efficiencies gained and a huge amount of dollars saved. It has been stated that if the banking industry operated on the level of technological sophistication that the healthcare system currently deploys, it would take three days to get cash from an ATM.

3. <u>An Aging Population:</u> This is in many ways a two-pronged problem. First, we are entering a period where the Baby Boomers, an absolutely huge demographic group in our population, are entering the middle to late years of their lives. This is also typically the time of life when people will be more avid consumers of healthcare resources. In fact, data shows that on average a great majority—nearly 75 percent—of the total dollars spent on a person's healthcare over his or her lifetime is spent during that person's last six months of life. This is a cost factor not much discussed because it really involves some complex ethical and moral questions around end of life issues. In addition, as people live longer, the healthcare dollars allocated to their care for their "retirement years" are inevitably inadequate, causing an additional drain and inefficiency in the system.

4. <u>Manual Processes:</u> There is a lack of automation and far too much manual processing of individual pieces of paper to even hope for efficiency. The entire healthcare system is designed around these manual processes and, in fact, it is this inefficiency that actually makes more money for the insurance companies in the long run due to their ability to delay and deny claims, earning more money

on those claim and premium dollars the longer they can keep from paying them out.

5. <u>Lack of Data Standards has plagued the industry</u>: In order for providers to be able to exchange information efficiently (or at all) there needs to be an accepted standard for formatting the records. The healthcare industry lags behind most other industries in defining and implementing standardized database records and coding systems. One would think that such standardized database records and coding systems would be desirable, especially in terms of processing claims within the system. Unfortunately, insurance companies decided that they did not want efficient mechanisms for processing claims. They wanted to control that process to their advantage. So even when they would agree on a method for coding claim forms for example, each company would come up with a way to bundle things under a particular code that would work to their advantage. This kind of jerry-rigging the system would result in widely disparate reimbursement rates from different companies for the same procedures, or certain procedures classified as "experimental" and not covered, when 90 percent of the other providers covered the same procedure without question.

Now our best chance at standardization, the implementation of International Classification of Diseases, 10th Revision, Clinical Modification (ICD-10-CM) provided by the Centers for Medicare and Medicaid Services (CMS) and the National Center for Health Statistics (NCHS), for medical coding and reporting in the United States. ICD-10 is underway but delayed. The deadline for the United States to begin using Clinical Modification ICD-10-CM for diagnosis coding and Procedure Coding System ICD-10-PCS for inpatient hospital procedure coding is currently October 1, 2014. The deadline was previously October 1, 2013. The basic structure of the ICD-10 code is the following: Characters 1-3 (the category of disease); 4 (etiology of disease); 5 (body part affected), 6 (severity of illness) and 7 (placeholder for extension of the code to increase specificity). Not only must new software be installed and tested, but medical practices must provide training for physicians, staff members, and administrators. They will also need to develop new practice policies and guidelines, and update paperwork and forms. Practices should also create crosswalks that will convert their most frequently used ICD-9 codes to the ICD-10 equivalents.

Efficiency in our healthcare system going forward depends on solving some of the issues mentioned above. And truthfully, these are big issues, but not issues that are too big to solve. Making significant progress toward reducing that 30 percent of inefficiency and waste really requires more than anything an agreement by the system that there is a problem, and then it becomes an issue of deploying the waiting and available solutions.

> Efficiency in our healthcare system going forward depends on solving some of the issues mentioned above. And truthfully, these are big issues, but not issues that are too big to solve.

At the core of this inefficiency problem is a triangle at the basis of every healthcare transaction. This triangle is made up of three "Ps": the Patient, the Physician (or Provider), and the Payer. The problem with this trio of players is that there really should be only two parties involved. When you look at that triangle from an efficiency standpoint, what does the Payer add to this equation other than delay, complexity, and additional cost? Nothing else—certainly no value or contribution to a quality outcome.

The Accountable Care Organization model, which we discuss in detail later and we believe needs to be a large part of the future of our healthcare system, essentially removes the Payer from the equation and seeks to emphasize the meaningful relationship between the Patient and the Provider. The accountable care organization model asks the question, why is the Payer in this equation at all? Why does the Physician have to have a relationship with the Payer? The Payer is not seeking medical advice. Why does the Patient have to deal with the Payer? He's seeking medical treatment. The accountable care organization says that the relationship that matters is between the physician and the patient. And the payment part of the equation should not be the focus of either the physician or the patient, it should just happen as a result of the transaction easily, seamlessly, without the need for a mountain of paper and claims processing personnel.

Another big contributor, at least temporarily, to the inefficiency of the system is actually the trend toward consumer-directed healthcare, and the cost-shifting that is already happening away from insurance companies and to individuals. Providers habituated to collecting fees for their services from insurance companies are now having to collect those fees from individuals. The inefficiency comes from the provider's ineptitude at collecting from individuals. On average, they write off 50 percent of the fees they try to collect from individuals. That's a huge annual number and we all pay for it in the form of higher fees.

Once the system has changed to the extent that payment for services happens at the time the service is rendered, electronically through the use of a multi-function / multi-purse benefit debit card, this aspect of inefficiency—physicians billing and collecting from patients—will all but disappear.

> Once the system has changed to the extent that payment for services happens at the time the service is rendered, electronically through the use of a multi-function / multi-purse benefit debit card, this aspect of inefficiency—physicians billing and collecting from patients—will all but disappear.

Healthcare Research and Development Spending

In so many ways in this country it seems as though we are quite spoiled. We are used to getting the best of everything and getting it immediately. That means the latest everything from the most incredible new flatscreen television to the latest smart phone to the hottest fashions. We don't want to wait and we won't settle for anything less than the best.

This philosophy, and the expectations it creates, applies across many, if not all aspects of our lives. When something is available and desirable (or because one of our friends has it), we tend to want it and we want it right now.

Not surprisingly, we take the same attitude with regard to our healthcare. Everything's got to be the latest and the greatest. We expect access to the newest, cutting edge drugs the minute they are available and the absolute latest in procedures and medical technology even if we really don't need them to improve overall outcomes. One thing is certain is – all of this cutting edge medicine comes with an extremely high price tag.

There are a huge number of surgical procedures performed each year—from Lasik eye surgery to some hip replacements—that are completely elective procedures. Now, we live in the land of the free, the home of capitalism, so choosing to have a particular procedure for any reason at all is not necessarily a problem for the healthcare system, so long as that procedure is being paid for by the patient. Unfortunately for us all, a huge percentage of these elective (i.e., non medically necessary) procedures are covered and paid for by medical insurance. Going back to our auto insurance analogy, that would be like your auto insurance paying for a new paint job on your car because you wanted to change the color or a new sound system because you didn't like the one that came with the car.

Ridiculous, right?

Again, we are here in the land of the free, the home of capitalism. The medical and pharmaceutical industries fund billions of dollars in research and development to make sure that they can satisfy our expectations for the latest and greatest. And they set the prices for these wonder drugs and procedures high enough to recoup their investment and make a handsome profit all because they know our healthcare system will cover and pay for it all. This is a huge factor in the spiraling cost of healthcare.

Part of our national discussion of the new healthcare horizon has to be about managing expectations—changing the "I want" mentality to one that's more aligned with what is really necessary for maintaining health and wellness.

There are two big questions that our policymakers need to answer and that discussion flies in the face of our "I want the best and I want it now" philosophy. The first is how should we fund medical and pharmaceutical research; how far should we go to chase the latest "wonder drug?" The second involves deciding whether the "system" is responsible for paying for clearly elective treatments and procedures, or whether more of that burden needs to fall to the person benefiting from those "optional" treatments.

The medical and pharmaceutical companies have extensive research and development departments that keep them on the cutting edge of healthcare. They spend billions of dollars each year to research the latest device, procedure, or wonder drug. It's a huge investment by these companies and recouping this investment is a huge driver of the high prices charged for these advances.

The truth is that many times the latest wonder drug may not deliver that much of an improvement over existing drugs or treatments. If a new drug costs 300 percent more than the existing drug does and only delivers a 25 percent better treatment outcome, should we always default as a system to wanting and paying for the latest and greatest? The question for our policymakers is whether this huge amount of money—essentially paid for by healthcare consumers in the form of high prices for drugs and procedures—would be better spent on existing treatments for various diseases? Or should there be a middle ground?

Many of the forward-thinkers in healthcare think we do in fact need a more conservative approach, one that matches cost with performance and efficacy. Where can we find examples of that kind of approach? Again we look to Germany for guidance.

In Germany, policymakers have decided that a new drug must be evaluated in terms of its potential efficacy before it can be presented to the system for reimbursement.

Because Germany has a multiple payer healthcare system that is administered by the government, they have faced the problem of managing expectations around new drugs and procedures head on. Germany has a government managed insurance scheme from which to pay for their entire population's healthcare. When a drug company—especially one based in Germany—wants to bring a new drug to the German market, it would attempt to charge a high price as they do in the United States. That pricing model—very high by German and European standards—was totally at odds with the available funds in their reimbursement system.

> Many of the forward-thinkers in healthcare think we do in fact need a more conservative approach, one that matches cost with performance and efficacy.

The government was faced with tough political and administrative challenges. On one hand, German citizens wanted to have access to the best treatment and medicines available, and the German government wanted to be able to provide the best for the quality of life for its citizens. However, allowing medical and pharmaceutical companies to charge these inflated prices would quickly result in essentially bankrupting their healthcare fund. Obviously, they needed to somehow control the costs. How could they accomplish both? They decided that the best way to control those costs on a system-wide basis was to apply an efficacy test to any new drug seeking approval and availability in Germany. They decided that a panel of qualified evaluators would determine how much more efficiency the new drug delivered as compared to the drug it was seeking to replace and then allow the company to charge a price that reflected that increased efficacy. For example, if the panel thought the new drug had 30 percent more benefit associated with it than the one it replaced, then the company could charge 30 percent more than the price of the current drug, not three or five times more.

One of the side effects of this policy is that German drug companies have moved their expensive "wonder drug" research out of Germany and have focused on making better generic versions of current drugs. And that has worked in Germany. The government has said that they are not going to pay for or encourage that kind of "wonder drug" research because as a healthcare system they simply can't afford to pay for it.

So the Germans, a people and a country with a long tradition of research and development in many areas, made a difficult decision that in the end will help preserve and improve the health of their citizenry. They made a decision to not be so far out on the leading edge of these wonder drugs that it would become literally the bleeding edge for their healthcare system.

It is obviously not an easy thing, politically, for policymakers to say to their constituents, "there are better drugs out there than we as a system can afford." That's a tough message to have to take home. It flies in the face of some of the myths and misconceptions discussed above, such as the "unlimited pool of healthcare dollars" and "the doctor can fix anything." They are betting that those wonder drugs will find a home elsewhere and that down the line, when they are more affordable, they (or generic equivalents) can be made available to their citizens. And so far that is the way it has worked.

Would policymakers in this country be willing to make that same decision here? Follow the German model for evaluating the efficacy of a new drug and base its reimbursement to the drug companies on the factor of improvement over existing drugs? The reasoning for doing it here is just as sound. The trick is obviously in overcoming the inertia of our "someone else pays for healthcare and I am entitled to the best drugs or treatment available regardless of cost" mentality. That would require tremendous resolve and strength of character from our policymakers. But given the severe and building cost pressures throughout the American healthcare system, what choice will we soon have to ignore these factors?

We expect the drugs available to us to be cutting edge. We expect the drugs to be continually improving, and their effectiveness to be ever-more impressive. We also expect the cost to be someone else's responsibility. We are at the end of our rope in terms of our healthcare system's ability to pay for those misconceptions and unrealistic expectations. So the question becomes how will we handle the same situation that Germany faced? It's here now, and the question is still unanswered.

> We expect the drugs available to us to be cutting edge. We expect the drugs to be continually improving, and their effectiveness to be ever-more impressive. We also expect the cost to be someone else's responsibility.

Elective surgical procedures—those that are performed but are not medically necessary—are another factor that is driving our healthcare costs higher. The question is not so much whether these procedures should be performed—there are plenty of good reasons for these treatments and procedures to be available—it's whether the healthcare system should pay for all or any part of these optional procedures.

Here's a not so far-fetched example. A 50-year-old man is an avid amateur soccer player and has been so for most of his adult life. He plays regularly and as a result is in very good shape for his age. He begins to notice soreness and problems with one of his knees and injures it in a minor way during a game. He goes to see his doctor who refers him to an orthopedic surgeon for an examination. The orthopedist confirms that the injury is minor but informs our soccer player that he has some structural issues with that knee that are the result of the increase wear and tear of years of playing soccer. The doctor is clear that, other than perhaps some stiffness and pain down the line, his knee will be fine for normal use. But if he continues to play soccer, he will likely be faced with some knee problems in the near future, perhaps a catastrophic injury because of the developing structural problems he detected. The orthopedist asks his patient if he wants to continue playing soccer. The patient says yes. The doctor tells him that he could perform a procedure now to fix that structural problem and "buy him" several more years on the soccer field. The patient says great, how much? The doctor says, this much and it'll be covered by your insurance.

That's great, right?

First, we should all be thrilled that this 50-year-old man is staying in good enough physical shape to play soccer at his age. But should our healthcare dollars go to pay for a procedure that is predominantly a lifestyle choice? His knee would have been fine, as the doctor said, for years to come. Who knows, his condition might have required a knee procedure at some point in the future and at that point the procedure would have been medically necessary for basic mobility.

The question is should we as a system really be paying for knee surgery or replacement for a 50-year-old person, someone who could wait until a later age for that procedure but really wants it for quality of life reasons?

And if that 50-year-old person needs another knee replacement at age 65 or 70, should the system pay for that one as well?

The availability of these elective procedures, paid for by insurance or Medicare, logically drives up the number of procedures that are performed and drives up the cost to the fee for service system dramatically.

The new technology behind these procedures is like the wonder drugs—once it's available, we want it immediately accessible. We want the benefit associated with them, whether that benefit is life-saving or just improves the quality of our lives. There's nothing wrong with that on its face; it simply comes down to the question of how much it costs and who pays the bill.

Connectivity, Missing Account, Manual Processes

Much has been written here and elsewhere about the tremendous inefficiency in our healthcare system, and the tremendous cost burden that inefficiency places on the system and on all of us as participants.

The degree of duplication and manual processes involved in every step of our healthcare system, from filling out a separate patient information form for every provider you visit, to the overly intricate manual coding of healthcare services by providers for insurance reimbursement is so huge that in order to assign a dollar cost to it, one would have to talk about multiple billions of dollars annually. It's simply staggering to imagine.

Tackling the inefficiency of the system must be done initially on at least two fronts: first, by eliminating paper-based manual record keeping, and second, by connecting all of the various sources—individual providers—to give a complete health picture for a particular patient.

> The degree of duplication and manual processes involved in every step of our healthcare system, from filling out a separate patient information form for every provider you visit, to the overly intricate manual coding of healthcare services by providers for insurance reimbursement is so huge that in order to assign a dollar cost to it, one would have to talk about multiple billions of dollars annually.

Our policymakers have begun by tackling the first issue, mandating that physicians adopt the technology to move all of their medical records to an electronic format by 2014 and providing incentives to those physicians who adopt said technology. It's a great first step in standardizing formats, reducing paperwork, and reducing errors. However, that mandate does not require connectivity for those physicians, so the issue of duplication and availability of records across the spectrum of providers is still a huge concern.

The benefit to the system of this connectivity and access to patient records across the healthcare industry is not only an efficiency benefit, it's also a huge quality of care issue. It's not hard to imagine this scenario: Someone is in a car accident. He is transported to the hospital in an unconscious or non-responsive state. He needs medical care and there is no way—unless he is a member of an organization such as Kaiser Permanente—to know whether that person has a serious drug allergy or a medical condition that would affect the decision making of that trauma team. The availability of a single health history of that person to providers with an authenticated need-to-know is a critical piece of the healthcare equation.

Some are quick to raise privacy issues surrounding the sharing of medical records. There are protections in place; the Health Insurance Portability and Accountability Act (HIPAA) provides significant protection. But the fact is that in order for our healthcare system to really work going forward, healthcare providers and consumers alike are going to have to get more comfortable with the idea of the availability on a need-to-know basis of medical records, not only for individual care reasons but also for the generic aggregation of data for cost control.

While the electronic records mandated in the Affordable Care Act address a real problem and will result in real financial benefits by reducing errors and human intervention, it is only part of the solution. But it does start us down the path to the rest of the solution.

Once the physicians have the technology—Electronic Medical Record (EMR), they have a standard they can use to populate a broader Personal Health Record (PHR). The PHR is then a standard for companies to use to aggregate standardized data for use both for tracking trends on a demographic basis, and also for use in developing products that a consumer can use to access this data for his own healthcare decision-making. This role as an aggregator and a developer of the consumer "dashboard" tool for accessing it is one several companies are poised to fill.

In many ways, the connectivity is the missing link. Consumers will need this aggregated data in order to fully participate in consumer-directed healthcare. The changes coming in our healthcare system will require the consumer to make more decisions on his own. Access to the information to make those decisions and even the ability to have one's own portable version of their health record is going to be increasingly important, bordering on critical.

> Many have said that this goal of a single, electronic, all-encompassing and even portable health record is too huge of a challenge, but in reality it is totally achievable.

Many have said that this goal of a single, electronic, all-encompassing and even portable health record is too huge of a challenge, but in reality it is totally achievable. Look at the changes in the banking and financial services industries over the past 20 years. Those industries have gone from paper-driven, parochial data systems to systems where you can view your entire financial picture on one screen and get cash in local currency with an ATM card on the other side of the world. The issue is not technological or logistical, it is emotional.

One thing is clear from the discussion in the previous sections: It's time to overhaul our healthcare industry in this country. It's time to re-chart the course of our healthcare destiny and restore some sanity and accountability to the runaway train of inefficiency and skyrocketing costs.

> One thing is clear from the discussion in the previous sections: it's time to overhaul our healthcare industry in this country.

Think back to that employer we talked about in Section I—the one who was less than thrilled when his insurance broker gave him the "great news" that his premiums were only going to increase by 12 percent next year. That annual message is only going to get worse. What happens in the next few years when that insurance broker comes back with the even worse news that premiums are only going up 40 percent? That's not outside the realm of possibility. We could really get there sooner rather than later. A 40 percent increase is something no employer can really handle even in the best of times. The chart below reflects the trend in rising insurance premiums over the past 13 years and provides a projection out to 2021 where insurance premium expense equals 31 percent of median family income.

Clearly he's done with the current system; he can't offer his employees the kind of benefits he would like to (or in some cases any benefits at all) without bankrupting his business. Cutting benefits is not a solution. He wants to change the rules, re-chart his own course. He's most likely done with that insurance broker. What options does he have in this era of mandated, guaranteed issue coverage for many under the Affordable Care Act?

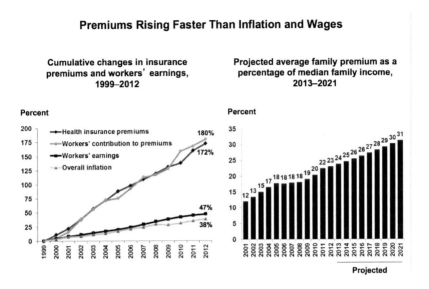

Premiums Rising Faster Than Inflation and Wages

Sources: (left) Kaiser Family Foundation/Health Research and Educational Trust, *Employer Health Benefits Annual Surveys, 1999–2012*; (right) authors' estimates based on CPS ASEC 2001–12, Kaiser/HRET 2001–12, CMS OACT 2012–21.

He needs to move away from his current, broken defined benefits system and switch to a defined contribution system—a system that will allow him to cap the amount of money he spends on his employee benefits and tailor that defined contribution to what is appropriate for his employees and his business. This is great news and will actually result in a better, more employee-directed and customized healthcare solution.

Studies indicate that currently 77 percent of employer-provided healthcare is based on the defined benefit model, where an employer offers, for example, Plan A or Plan B from one or maybe two providers like BlueCross. Studies tend to indicate that within the next five years there will be almost a 180-degree flip, resulting in 69 percent of employers having moved to a defined contribution model. That's a huge turnaround, and a huge statement from employers on just how unworkable the current system is.

Basic Concepts of Defined Contribution

There are fundamental healthcare changes ahead involving a shift from traditional "defined benefit" plans to "defined contribution" plans. This shift is similar in nature to the historical change from defined benefit pension plans to more consumer-centric defined contribution – 401K retirement plans.

> There are fundamental healthcare changes ahead involving a shift from traditional "defined benefit" plans to "defined contribution" plans.

With defined benefit healthcare, an institutional purchaser, such as an employer determines what range of services it will cover and then seeks, or creates a plan that will provide those services for an acceptable price. It has become increasingly difficult for institutional purchasers to sustain a defined benefit approach as a steady stream of emerging healthcare treatments and technologies requires an equally steady stream of decisions about which ones will be covered by the plan. Moreover, from an economic standpoint it has become nearly impossible to provide such benefits in the face of rising healthcare inflation and increasingly impotent cost-cutting tools.

Newer versions of defined contribution plans, commonly implemented as "consumer-directed healthcare benefits" feature financial accounts, in conjunction with a scaled down traditional healthcare plan – typically a high deductible, catastrophic plan, on which the beneficiary can draw. The account might be a flexible spending account (FSA) or health savings account (HSA) in which employees set aside their own pre-tax money to cover expenses of designated sorts, including healthcare. Or it can be a health reimbursement account (HRA) that an employer funds, or some combination of spending account types.

Within this spending account approach, employees can simply purchase a conventional health plan or, in more interesting versions, buy individual services and products or use the funds to cobble together a health plan to suit one's preferences. One basic approach involves the employee using some of the funds to purchase a high-deductible insurance plan, and then draws on the remainder to pay for individual expenses that arise throughout the year, ideally with the freedom to roll over any funds left from one year into future years. The spending account might be sufficient to cover the entire deductible, or it might require the employee to ante up some expenses out of pocket.

Limitless Possibilities in Plan Design

The possible variations of defined contribution plans are endless. In addition to providing access to plan, medical, and provider information and facilitating consumer enrollment into their chosen defined contribution plan, some plans also help enrollees keep track of expenditures as they draw on their spending account for various services and plan for future needs. In some plans, money not used during one year can be rolled over for use in future years, although the exact details depend on funding sources and applicable tax rules. In cases where enrollees spend all the money in their spending account and still need care, or where they use out-of-area services, traditional insurance coverage takes over. That coverage might begin immediately, or enrollees might be required to spend some of their own money as a "bridge" before catastrophic insurance coverage begins.

In sum, self-directed plans permit enrollees to become their own health advocate, benefits manager, and utilization reviewer, deciding which services are worth purchasing at what price and from whom, and managing the money in their account to promote prudent purchasing of the healthcare they value.

Top 10 Advantages of Defined Contribution Plans

For employers, the obvious advantage of defined contribution is the ability to limit expenditures at the outset, rather than promising a level of benefits and then hoping to find an affordable price. At the same time, beneficiaries face an obvious (potential) disadvantage. Because the employer no longer accepts increased costs to support a given level of care, beneficiaries may end up with whatever lesser level of care the defined sum will buy. However, that downside is hardly the final analysis. For one thing, even defined benefit plans do not ensure a given level of benefits. Worsening economic conditions have prompted many employers to make marked cuts from one year to the next. Even within a given year, enrollees cannot be sure that their benefit levels actually remain intact. So long as healthcare contracts provide only vague promises to cover "medically necessary" services, health plans can steadily erode the actual level of coverage within any given plan simply by declaring this or that service to be unnecessary. On the other hand, the advantages of defined contribution plans — particularly the spending account versions — can be substantial.

1.   Availability: When patients pay for the daily, mundane healthcare expenses out of a dedicated account they face no significant financial barriers to accessing care. Assuming that the dedicated health account is sufficient to cover most routine expenses plus purchase a catastrophic plan, even an otherwise impecunious patient need not forego ordinary care on account of cost.

Reciprocally, patients themselves enjoy the financial savings of prudent purchasing. In conventional plans, when coverage for a service is refused as "unnecessary," it is plans, employers, or governments, not patients, who pocket the savings.

2. Accountability: Patients have virtually complete control over which services they receive, at least for routine expenses covered directly by the personal savings account. There is no need for an HMO or other health plan to dictate which tests, treatments, or drugs patients may receive, or to deny coverage for nonstandard services such as acupuncture or laser vision correction, because patients cover these directly from their own account. Self-control replaces external control.

> For employers, the obvious advantage of defined contribution is the ability to limit expenditures at the outset, rather than promising a level of benefits and then hoping to find an affordable price.

Admittedly, the control exerted by managed care organizations (MCOs) over specific health benefits has loosened in recent years. And yet that loosening has come at the cost of substantial premium increases that employers are unlikely to shoulder for long during an economic downturn. If so, then MCOs wanting to stay in business will be forced to reinitiate significant control over medical/spending decisions, to place pervasive monetary caps on various kinds of services, or to find some other way to clamp down once again on the rising costs of care. If costs must be contained, and patients are not incentivized to do it for themselves, someone will do it for them.

3. <u>Consistency</u>: Patients, likewise, control which providers they see because the patient, not the plan, directly incurs the expense. Patients can choose any physician or specialist, any time they wish, without begging for gatekeeper approval. More important, patients are free to continue in a physician-patient relationship of their choosing. One of the more egregious flaws of mid-1990s managed care was frequent changes in provider networks. Sometimes they occurred when employers shifted employees to a new health plan with a different provider network, and other times when health plans discontinued contracts with particular providers or provider groups. Either way, many patients and physicians were deeply distressed by being forced to sever longstanding relationships simply because this year's plan had changed. Such disruptions can be medically and economically counterproductive. Studies show that continuity of relationships yields better outcomes, lower costs and greater satisfaction for patients and physicians alike (Barr 1995, Ferber 1996, Roulidis and Schulman 1994, Epstein 1995).

Health plans, too, can benefit when patients remain with a particular plan over time. When patients frequently shift from one plan to the next, plans that provide excellent care for chronic diseases such as diabetes can suffer significant financial losses. This is because years in the future, some other plan will enjoy the financial rewards of this plan's forward-looking preventive care. However, once patients have the power to choose their own health plan, including choosing the same plan from one year to the next, plans have an incentive to please the patient rather than the employer and to attract that patient's continued business. Ultimately, such relationships might even make multi-year contracts possible, thereby enhancing plans' ability to improve service and control long-range costs.

4. Integrity: Once patients are financially free to contract directly with the physician of their choice to buy the services they want, the physician-patient relationship can be on a sounder ethical footing than in many MCOs. Physicians need not labor under odious external micromanagement, nor spend endless hours begging and haranguing permission to provide the simplest interventions. Neither do health plans need to pay physicians insidious incentives for withholding care. In the routine care covered by a spending account, the only financial relationship is between the physician who recommends an intervention and the patient who receives and directly pays for it. If the physician says, "You don't need the costly brand-name drug," the patient need not wonder about ulterior motives. And if the physician says, "You really do need this test," the patient knows the only incentive is the traditional fee-for-service incentive encouraging physicians to do more than is needed. However, when the physician knows that any excess comes from the patient's own account, and not from a rich, distant insurance company, the professional ethics of personal fidelity are far more likely to shape his recommendations. Moreover, patients who are spending from their own account are more likely to ask whether something is really needed, whether it can wait or whether there is a more conservative alternative.

5. Accuracy: Opportunities for fraud are greatly reduced. When third parties cover the expenses and the bills are breathtakingly complex, patients have little reason to scrutinize bills to ensure every entry is correct. Indeed, third-party payment encourages providers to continue their inscrutable billing practices so that errors are not readily noticeable. In contrast, when patients pay their own bills immediately after services, they know whose financial account is being drained and they know (or can immediately ask) whether they are being properly charged. Moreover, even providers who

might be inclined to cheat a large, anonymous insurer may be much more reluctant to defraud a patient with whom they have a personal relationship.

6. Efficiency: Spending accounts can yield administrative cost savings. When patients are empowered to make their own decisions, there is no need for costly claims processing procedures, eligibility determinations, utilization review or appeals following denials of coverage. Patients can simply present a debit card to the physician, pharmacist or whomever, and payment is instant. In the process, providers need not wait weeks to months, nor file multiple claims, before they are paid.

7. Choice: Patients who want extravagant or nonstandard care are not imposing on other people, at least within the ambit of the spending account. If patients want the costliest drugs, they pay out of their own funds, not common resources. At the same time, the fact that the patient pays means that most decisions will be considered more carefully than they are at present. It is easy to demand antibiotics for a viral illness or insist on the expensive new drug advertised on the television when others bear the costs. It is another thing when the cost of that drug comes directly out of one's own funds. By the same token, with more prudent decision making it may even be possible to avoid some of the problems of medical excess, such as the emergence of resistant organisms that result from the overuse of antibiotics.

8. Advances: When health plans no longer need to govern myriad small expenses, they are free to focus on the important realm: costly care for people with serious illness or injury, i.e., the people who dip into their catastrophic coverage. As of 1996, 1 percent of patients consumed 27 percent of total health expenditures, while

the top 10 percent of patients consumed nearly 70 percent, and the top 30 percent consumed 90 percent. This picture has not changed significantly over several decades (Berk and Monheit 2001:12). Plans need to stop niggling over minor matters and take the lead in assessing costly new technologies and innovative interventions to ensure that evidence-based approaches will make the best possible uses of the great majority of common funds.

9. Portability: Defined contribution approaches are considerably more portable than many current health plans. Particularly when self-insured employers establish their own distinctive set of benefits and provider networks, workers who change jobs usually begin a completely new plan, often with new providers. In contrast, because defined contribution plans generally permit enrollees to choose their own providers and treatments, at least at the lower levels within the deductible range, they offer considerably more continuity across job changes.

10. Participation: Patients who control their own dollars have considerably greater reason to be informed participants in their own care. When employers choose the health plan, and when plans determine which care is "necessary" from what kind of provider in which setting, patients have relatively little reason or opportunity to become full partners in their care. Active participation in one's care can, in itself, be medically beneficial (Kaplan et al. 1996; Kaplan, Greenfield, and Ware 1989).

Admittedly patients can make mistakes, such as to forego useful care in order to save money. However, it is not clear that patients' decisions about which care is (un)necessary will be any worse than the denials now issued by health plans, often for medically dubious reasons. Moreover, it is not always so clear when a given intervention is actually useful, let alone "necessary." The science behind the guidelines and recommendations issued by plans and by providers is often scanty in both quality and quantity, and one day's gospel becomes the next day's heresy with surprising facility. When patients are restored to a mutually trusting relationship with their physicians, and with increasing access to solid medical information, they may be more amenable to persuasion about which care is most important and thereby worthy of dipping into their medical spending account. Also, because defined contribution funds can be dedicated to healthcare and made immediately available, patients have far less reason to forego important care than in standard plans requiring patients to pay deductibles out of pocket for first-dollar health expenses.

> The time has arrived to integrate patients into the picture and restore to them the power and responsibility of the purse that can, in turn, permit them the freedom to shape their care according to their own values.

In the final analysis, the past decade's extraordinary turbulence has taught some important lessons. It has been a time of trial and error in which the medical community's failure to constrain its spending gave way to a business orientation that failed to appreciate clinical realities. Doctors did not make good business people, and business people did not make good doctors. Still, the transition is hardly complete and we may yet see a happier ending. The time has arrived to integrate patients into the picture and restore to them the power and responsibility of the purse that can, in turn, permit them the freedom to shape their care according to their own values.

Three really significant benefits of the defined contribution model for employers and employees are:

1. It enables employees to make the healthcare choices that fit best with their individual long-term financial plans. In a private exchange model allowing comparison shopping for health and ancillary insurance benefits, the range of choices for the employee can become far broader and more extensive than possible under the old defined benefits model.

2. It establishes a basis of accountability on the part of each individual for their own wellness. The system can provide the educational resources and calculators to help them realize the long-term cost savings and rewards for that commitment to wellness.

3. It establishes the basis for financial accountability and cost control for employers. The defined contribution model is so much simpler and predictable for both the employer and employee.

However, the shift to a defined contribution model is truly only part of the solution. What about our example employer's employees? He can't simply tell them "Here's the company's contribution to your healthcare, there are lots of insurance companies out there, good luck!"

Part of the Affordable Care Act is the mandate that by January of 2014 virtually everyone in this country must be enrolled in, or covered by, at least a minimum benefit set healthcare plan. For those persons not covered by employer provided healthcare—including the self-employed and the unemployed—each state will be required to offer its own healthcare plan options to its citizens to meet the enrollment mandate. The mechanism mandated by the Act to enroll those individuals without company-provided healthcare is called a "public exchange." The best way to visualize an exchange is to think about such marketplaces as Priceline.com or Expedia.com in the travel industry. These are in essence shopping malls where hundreds of travel options and providers can be compared.

The public exchanges are where each state will create its own electronic tool that will present a menu of options and allow state residents to make their healthcare choices and, if they qualify, receive a grant, subsidy, or credit for their plan. Should the state decide for whatever reason not to comply with the federal mandate, the federal government will provide its own federal public exchange to the state. Again, the goal here is to provide a mechanism for everyone to be covered, and therefore eliminate or minimize the high cost that the uninsured place on the system.

Just as the states will set up their public exchanges, private employers making the switch to a defined contribution model will want the same kind of "shopping mall" for their employees—a private exchange. In the example, the employer will want to sponsor an environment that is helpful and comfortable for the employees to "shop" for their healthcare needs.

These private exchanges are really the future of how to implement, organize and administer employer-provided healthcare. The exchanges can be as comprehensive and rich as the employer desires, whatever fits the employer's particular corporate culture. The exchange can also be used to enroll in benefits other than just major medical, such as dental, vision, life insurance, disability insurance, or long-term care. The exchange could also handle specialized (and increasingly common) health savings accounts and even handle the COBRA (continuation of benefits post-termination) needs of an employee who leaves the company.

So how are these private exchanges created and administered? A private exchange sponsor is contracted by the employer to create and administer the exchange, performing the functions that the employer's human relations department and/or and insurance broker might traditionally perform. The firm would present a monthly consolidated bill for all services as opposed to the barrage of monthly bills from individual providers that employers currently face.

> Private exchanges are really the future of how to implement, organize and administer employer-provided healthcare.

So, what's the key to getting all of this started? Can we accomplish this revolution in our lifetimes?

Technology and connectivity are the keys.

Advances in technology have effectively enabled new ways to engage consumers in this long-term view of health benefits and retirement. Along with those advances, increasing transparency in pricing, program features, and the ability to educate consumers on their healthcare options will help enable some of this change in consumer behavior. These factors will help enable us to move into more of a true free-market type environment, where we can embrace real competitiveness. This will eventually provide a wider and deeper range of individual choices and perhaps work to drive down costs.

The touch point for this revolution—the interface where the consumer really begins to take control—is the exchange, for its ability to present prices and features on a truly comparative basis.

> Advances in technology have effectively enabled new ways to engage consumers in this long-term view of health benefits and retirement.

At first, the exchanges and the tools we use to access them will center on enrollment and comparing premium cost. As they evolve, they will become much more than a premium calculator. Consumers will also be able to weigh the different coverage options that are available within each plan. It will weigh the different exclusions that are available. It will weigh the different co-pays that will be levied under the terms of the policy. It will allow consumers to drill down further and further on the information side of the exchange to really determine if a particular plan meets his needs from a coverage standpoint as well as a budgetary one.

The federal government has mandated that each state set up its own public exchange. Each state has the opportunity—whether seized or not—to set up an exchange according to its own laws that will allow insurance companies to present plans to the public and allow those people who wish to and are not covered by an employer's plan to enroll and purchase coverage on the exchange. The enrollment process will be similar to the process we walked through at the beginning of this book. Each person will enter his or her personal information, and then the system will determine whether or not that individual is eligible for a tax credit, eligible for an outright subsidy or eligible for Medicaid payment expansion to pay for the some or all of the coverage. If the state chooses not to set up its own exchange, the federal government will impose a federal exchange template to serve as the state public exchange. The law mandates that each state have an exchange up and running by January 1, 2014.

The federal government is paying the states to set up the exchanges, and once the exchanges are set up it then becomes the state's responsibility to figure out how to pay for them going forward. Different states are taking different approaches and some states are simply refusing to comply. It remains to be seen just how effectively the mandates can be enforced.

As of the date of this writing, as many as 17 states have decided to pursue setting up their own exchanges this year; seven states have decided to partner with the federal government. The remaining 26 states may adopt the federal exchange template and a few will likely refuse to comply with the mandate completly. Those states will simply sit back and wait to see what the federal government does. This approach will set the stage for a historic test of American federalism and state/federal relations.

When the idea of the exchanges was being formulated, the federal government assumed an overwhelming majority of the states would develop their own exchange models. The thought was that maybe five states would end up with the federal exchange, and 45 states would do it on their own. It was not considered that only a minority of states would opt to build their own. So it appears that the federal government will be responsible for establishing possibly a majority of the state exchanges.

All of this activity surrounding the development of the federal and state exchanges is happening at a fast pace. These exchanges need to be up and running for enrollment by October 2013 for the 2014 plan year. They may not get it all done.

Because the exchange concept has been publicly sanctioned by the Affordable Care Act, it is gaining more and more currency in the private market, and we think it will continue to gain traction and build momentum as the new paradigm for making better health choices.

> Because the exchange concept has been publicly sanctioned by the Affordable Care Act, it is gaining more and more currency in the private market, and we think it will continue to gain traction and build momentum as the new paradigm for making better health choices.

We think that the health choice component of the exchanges will really help to change behaviors because there will be rewards for that changed behavior—not hollow promises of better things to come, but tangible benefits and incentives that a consumer will be able to see within the private exchange interface. We believe that consumers will embrace these lifestyle choices that can really bring down our long-term health cost. Whether those changes involve smoking cessation, weight loss, better diet and fitness, or adherence to whatever regimen one needs to follow. It is the same revolution that the financial services industry went through—tremendous changes in data aggregation and then presenting that data to consumers in such a way that people could really get a better handle on what their financial situation was for retirement, characterized by individual choice and reward.

For most Americans this kind of transparency was truly revolutionary in opening their eyes to the potential (and reality) of their financial future, and actually allowed them to view and understand the ramifications of their financial decision-making.

Because we all pay for healthcare we all have the ability and responsibility to do our part to keep those costs down. Making better health choices for our own individual situations is a huge part of that responsibility.

Several private enterprises are poised to deliver exactly this level of experience for our healthcare—the technology already exists as does the consumer portal. Connectivity and the aggregation of data across providers is the challenge facing all of us in healthcare. That connectivity and data sharing is how we take the next big leap in fixing our healthcare system.

In a world where we have countless smart phone applications available for anything you could possibly imagine, we need an application—not tied to or selling the products of a particular company, but neutral, agnostic—that provides an individual with information about his health status, his latest test results, and what actions he can take to improve his health status. The consumer can set health goals and track progress toward achieving them on a smart phone or computer.

One thing we know for sure about nearly every segment of our population is that internet-connected computers and smart phones have tremendous market penetration. Some studies put the market penetration of smart phones at more than 50 percent of the population. Some studies conclude that 90 percent of the population has at least some kind of connected device—even those segments of the population that live below the poverty level.

This is all encouraging news to those trying to revolutionize how we look at healthcare and healthy living. We actually have a viable way to reach the people we need to reach. It's critical to be able to deliver information and program options on as many different platforms as possible.

But even with the Affordable Care Act's mandate of nearly universal coverage and the revolutionary technology around making sound healthcare choices, there will still be those who manage to stay out of the system.

> As we discussed earlier, there are currently an estimated 49 million people who have no current health insurance.

As we discussed earlier, there are currently an estimated 49 million people who have no current health insurance. Government projections are that as a result of the Affordable Care Act, 32 million of them will be brought into the system by 2022. That leaves 17 million people (just under 5 percent of the U.S. population) who, for whatever reason, are still not being covered. Obviously, this projection is good news and bad news—a great number of people who are currently not paying into the system will be doing so, but it also leaves a significant number still outside the system. This number is large enough to overwhelm emergency rooms and continue to do major financial damage to what will hopefully be a recovering healthcare system.

So who are these 17 million people and why aren't they covered? There will be 17 million different reasons—"I can't access the tools," "I didn't have a car that day," "my brother-in-law didn't show up to take me down to the office"—any combination of reasons. It could be that they don't even know about the mandate. For as widespread and ubiquitous being connected has become in our society, there still are people who are not connected. And there's a segment of the population that even if they are connected and do know about the mandates they could benefit from, won't address it because for whatever reason they don't want to reveal themselves to the system. Members of this segment will likely never be reachable—they have their own cost/benefit analysis they do to decide if a benefit from one side of the government is better than the price that they may have to pay for exposure to another side of the government.

The uninsured will always be a problem with any healthcare system— the challenge for policymakers going forward as they tweak and adjust legislation like the Affordable Care Act is to keep that number of uninsured to as small a number as possible.

Looking Abroad for Solutions

As we look to lay the cornerstone and define the parameters of a new and viable healthcare system in this country, there are significant lessons to be learned and examples to follow in other countries around the world.

A lot has been written—and much of it negative—about healthcare systems in Canada and England. The "socialized medicine" and "wait for care" labels applied to those systems where the government is the healthcare provider and payer. The stigma attached to these systems is significant in the United States. Segments of our population refuse to allow anymore of what they consider government intrusion into their lives, and thus supporting the adoption of a government operated single payer healthcare system in this country is not reasonably foreseeable. Similarly, the Canadian model's "wait for care" reputation is equally distasteful in a country where we are famous for our love of instant gratification. Although there may be aspects of both systems that can be emulated here, holding them up as examples of something to be implemented in this country does not seem to be a viable option.

Germany, on the other hand is an interesting example to study because it is a government-administered system with a universal mandate for health insurance: everyone must be covered by insurance. There is both a public healthcare system and a private system. Germans are either in the public system or the private system. Enrollment in the public system is about 90 percent of the population and 10 percent are in the private healthcare system. If you're in the public system, there are organizations set up to manage the health insurance needs of segments of the population—these can be set up by labor unions, companies or sometimes by region.

The German system was outlined in the 1880's. German citizens enrolled in the public healthcare system have a choice of scores of different private insurance providers and like here, there is an annual open enrollment period where they can change providers. All of the insurance providers in the German system are private insurance providers and they compete vigorously against one another in their respective marketplaces, whether they be regional or national.

The fact that Germany's healthcare system is built of only private insurers might bring out some skepticism as to the wisdom of using their system as an example, given the dismaying performance of private insurance companies in our current system. But it is a good example for us for one simple reason: it works.

It's not perfect, but it works.

Why does it work? Clearly, the strict government oversight and administration, coupled with cost controls have lead to affordability and accountability in the system. The other factor is, of all things, cooperation and integration between all of the parties to make the system work. There is also the fact that the system has been tweaked and improved over its nearly 130 years of operational history.

Perhaps the biggest lesson from the German system for our policymakers is the level of cooperation and integration they have been able to achieve within the network of private insurance providers. We believe that the Affordable Care Act will be an excellent means to begin to foster that cooperation and integration here. In addition, the mechanism of the exchange will quickly become a powerful driver in convincing providers and employers alike that transparency can have real bottom-line, economic benefits.

Some have said that the Affordable Care Act was rushed through and enacted without a clear plan of how its goals and mandates were going to be achieved. We don't believe that's the case at all. This country has had as a part of its political discourse for the past 100 years discussion of the need for widespread healthcare reform. Other countries have been able to do this. The legislation itself may have been a bit ambitious in terms of its short-term goals, but long term it is the direction we need to be headed.

The challenge for us as a country is that our system requires massive amounts of change in order to remain viable, much less improve. In 1981, the United States Government devoted 10 percent of its budget to healthcare expenditures. Today it's 22 percent and without modification, by 2030 it's projected to be 33 percent. With more than

$2.5 trillion in expenditures annually in healthcare there is a huge economic impact on the country as well as on its citizens.

The path through this period of change is most definitely through more information, more transparency, and more integration of available healthcare options. We believe that private companies ready to be the neutral, comprehensive resource for employers and individuals will prosper in the coming environment.

> The challenge for us as a country is that our system requires massive amounts of change in order to remain viable, much less improve. In 1981, the United States Government devoted 10 percent of its budget to healthcare expenditures. Today its 22 percent and without modification, by 2030 it's projected to be 33 percent.

The bottom line is that our healthcare system can be rescued through technology and data aggregation, which utilizes an interface that allows employers and consumers to make comparative choices. Companies that are ahead of the pack in providing the means for employers to offer their employees a better range of choices and the fully integrated package to manage, administer and pay for those choices should have a bright future.

SECTION IV
TRANSFORMATIVE HEALTHCARE MODEL

Accountable Care Organization

Amidst significant change and turmoil — new insurance plan types, continued downward pressure on provider rates, diminished and sometimes negative margins for Medicare and Medicaid payments, cost shifting, increased cost accountability for consumers and limited/dubious quality measurements or controls – U.S. healthcare costs have continued to rise at unsustainable rates. It is clear that the standard fee-for-service healthcare model is not working. The economic picture, combined with the impetus of healthcare reform, mandates substantial cost reduction efforts, and an increased emphasis on care quality. Put simply, there is a strong need to create a more competitive U.S. healthcare market. Enter: accountable care organizations (ACOs), one of the new business models enhanced by healthcare reform.

Creating a More Competitive U.S. Healthcare System

Under the ACO approach, physicians and hospitals would band together and take ownership for quality of care and overall annual healthcare spending for their patients – and, to some degree, would be compensated based on annual performance measures (such as resource use and quality targets). Ultimately, the model is intended to foster collaboration and increased focus on delivering patient value and reducing overall healthcare costs. The ACO concept holds much promise – long-term fiscal responsibility, increased patient safety and quality of care, more equitable cost/compensation models, increased efficiency, and a truly patient-centered focus. But many obstacles and uncertainties remain. There will be significant infrastructure costs to integrate physicians. There are varying opinions about the rules and implications. And the return-on-investment (ROI) model remains unproven.

Success Hinges on Engaging Consumers

One thing is certain, however – the patient must be paramount in the ACO model in order for it to be successful. In today's healthcare environment consumers are increasingly responsible for the cost of their own healthcare – this despite the fact that most consumers, as a result of a lifetime of PPO coverage and limited out-of-pocket obligations, have been conditioned not to consider the cost implications of their healthcare decisions. The reduction of overall healthcare costs is dependent, in part, upon consumers making more thoughtful and economically responsible healthcare choices. Positive health outcomes are also largely dependent upon consumer behaviors – such as following prescribed treatment protocols and making healthy choices that prevent the onset of chronic disease.

With incentives for positive health outcomes and overall cost reduction, ACOs will need to place significant emphasis on empowering consumers to make informed choices – for everything from choosing a health plan, to managing their family's financial health, to making healthcare and treatment decisions. Historically, a lack of transparency regarding price and physician quality information has made it challenging for consumers to compare prices and services and to plan for the cost of their care.

And health literacy amongst Americans is surprisingly low, which contributes to an abundance of chronic issues such as obesity. ACOs must find ways to break down these barriers and serve up a variety of information on cost, benefits, quality, wellness, clinical information, and more.

This information must be served up in a fashion that is interactive and engaging – such as videos, calculators, forums, quizzes, FAQ documents,

OVERDOSE: Your Health, My Money

and more. And it must be delivered through the channels consumers desire, be it online or via a mobile device. Consumers today are used to having information at their fingertips. Right from their mobile device, they can perform a variety of activities – from communicating with friends/family to interacting via social media to paying bills, to researching almost any subject via the Web. Consumers will have the same expectations for their healthcare.

With patients' long-term well-being in mind, portability, too, must be a key focus. ACOs must arm consumers with tools to manage their healthcare spending accounts, plan coverage and personal health information – even as they change employers, health insurance plans, financial institutions, and physicians.

It's clear the ACO model has the potential to create positive change in healthcare delivery and management. New products, technology, administrative and operational platforms, and resources will be critical to support this healthcare transformation. And at the center of the equation stands the consumer (patient). ACOs must not forget about the vital importance of empowering consumers. Indeed, it will be critical to the success of the ACO model.

The new model for healthcare in this country, as it emerges from all of the changes being imposed on our healthcare system by the Affordable Care Act and other influences, is really a transformative healthcare model where the desired end result is a fully functional, efficient, consumer driven, and paid for healthcare model that stresses proactive behavior.

This transformation from a broken, dysfunctional system of over-inflated costs and mind-numbing waste and inefficiency has a core concept and business model as its cornerstone: the ACO. Just how would this model work in the context of the current healthcare landscape?

Under the ACO approach, physicians and hospitals work together to take ownership for the quality of care and overall healthcare spending for their patients, and, to some degree, would be compensated based on annual performance measures to that end. Ultimately, the model is intended to foster collaboration and cooperation, and to increase focus on delivering patient value in reducing overall healthcare costs. The ACO concept holds much promise for long-term fiscal responsibility, increased efficiencies and a true patient-centered focus.

An ACO will most likely be made up of either physician groups that have banded together or a hospital and a physician group that have come together to form an organization that is accountable for managing the risk for whatever population they serve. This could be a geographic population or it could be an employee population. An interesting trend that we are seeing is physician groups across state lines are banding together, driven down that path to gain advantages in purchasing supplies, equipment, technology, and even administrative services—things that they can leverage to their advantage as a larger group.

The banking industry is a good example of these kinds of interstate alliances. When legislation was passed that allowed banks to engage in interstate activities, we frequently saw alliances form across the country that eliminated duplication and increased each individual bank's leverage and efficiency. As an example, cash is available worldwide from any ATM with any debit card regardless of issuer or the underlying network infrastructure.

The Affordable Care Act is very supportive of the concept of an ACO and defines it as "a group of providers or suppliers, or a network of groups often affiliated with a hospital, that are jointly responsible for the cost and quality of the healthcare provided to Medicare beneficiaries because they receive bonuses when they provide exceptional or low-cost care and are penalized for low-quality or high-cost care."

While that definition specifically mentions a Medicare context, the government is clearly trying to encourage the scenario where a group of providers, suppliers, or a network affiliated with a hospital jointly takes responsibility for the cost and quality of healthcare because they can receive bonuses and benefits when they succeed.

The word "accountable" is the key here. Using the Medicare context above, the federal government would reward or by extension penalize an accountable care organization based on how it performed, which would be measured by the standards set for Medicare patients. It's a logical and intuitive way to ensure successful and cost-effective care.

It is important to note that this emerging accountable care organization paradigm does not necessarily need to have an insurance company as part of the equation. The role of the insurance company would be to share the risk and forestall the occurrence of unacceptable losses. This can be accomplished by the organization purchasing generally available stop-loss insurance, so while you may see insurers and healthcare providers come together, it's not the only way.

We are already seeing examples of these accountable care organizations being developed. Some have even been flourishing for quite some time. Take Kaiser Permanente, a healthcare organization based on the West Coast. They are, in essence, a health insurance company combined with a network of hospitals and clinics. They are vertically integrated and in an interesting place to embrace the changes ahead.

> We are already seeing examples of these accountable care organizations being developed. Some have even been flourishing for quite some time.

Kaiser has embraced the concept of accountable care and the evolution toward wellness; they embrace preventative care and consumer choice. They have built in to their model significant incentives and rewards to ensure that their patient population is well cared for. They run a very efficient system and have great data aggregation and transparency to medical records within their system. For the most part, people are more engaged in their own healthcare at Kaiser and while it does resemble an HMO approach in that there is very little referral outside of their own care providers, it is very definitely a model to watch. Kaiser's transition to the new healthcare paradigm will be much less painful than other companies.

Another example is a situation we observed in Minnesota where a health insurance company acquired a large regional healthcare system. The insurance company most likely looked at the acquisition as a way to leverage the infrastructure of the healthcare network to sign up more policyholders, but in some ways they have created the beginnings of an ACO. And while it is not necessary to have an insurance company be part of an ACO (in most cases it is not desirable), it can have its benefits and make the integration easier.

So the ACO can actually accomplish its goals without an insurance company involved in the equation. A private exchange sponsor could work with the hospital/physician group or employer group, facilitate the stop-loss insurance, and then apply its existing tools to accommodate the consumer experience. Several companies in fact have such a model and they possess all the elements necessary to have this type of organization up and running.

One type of ACO solution creates a third party administrator relationship with the hospital/physician group. The risk transfer takes place as a result of purchasing stop-loss insurance. Managing the network physicians and/or practice groups that are involved in providing the care is handled by a back office operation. It does the administration and the calls. The hospital/physician group gets the benefit programs, the online technology necessary in an integrated database to provide all of these services, the call center, and the claims-paying aspect of actually exchanging money for services performed.

This accountable care scenario is accomplished without the additional layer of administration and cost of one or more insurance providers. It is a system that can operate more efficiently because there isn't an insurance company in the middle of the decision process—a decision process that really should only be between the physician and the patient. Without the insurance element in the equation, there are fewer parties, less paper, and less delay. There is more efficiency in terms of the time that it takes to deliver the care and, therefore, all measures of efficiency are enhanced.

There's one other key area where we believe that the ACO paradigm will have a positive effect on our healthcare system. One of the major flaws in our current healthcare system is its dependence on the "fee-for-service" business model, a model that is not prevalent elsewhere. It's a model where doctors are incented to do more rather than less, whether or not it qualitatively affects the patient's outcome. This results in situations where doctors are frequently ordering tests that don't necessarily provide information or prescribing treatments that are not necessarily going to increase the quality of care or the desirability of the outcome, but will result in higher fee generation.

Much has already been written about the impact of the tort system and concomitant cost of medical malpractice insurance and it is not our intention to review that data. However, the key point is that the threat of negligence lawsuits against doctors results in more rather than fewer tests and procedures since one of the defenses to negligence is to demonstrate that "everything possible" was done whether or not that resulted in a higher quality of care. It does conveniently play into a "fee-for-service" compensation model. The current medical malpractice landscape clearly raises the cost of American healthcare, perhaps significantly. Despite the political difficulty, tort reform will be a major component to repair our healthcare system. Again, the problem has been confronted and effectively addressed overseas. As we progress, real cost containment will mandate reform.

We think that ACO's will move away from the "fee-for-service" model and move toward an outcome-based model, accepting fees based on the outcome and the quality of the care that was delivered. This model is in fact consistent with the goals as stated in the Affordable Care Act.

A Rise In Healthcare Consumerism

There is a long-overdue rise in consumerism with regard to our healthcare system, and patients are beginning to think about their healthcare the same way that they think every other service that they purchase in their daily lives. We think that this is a great thing, a transformative thing and it's about time!

With the coming changes in the healthcare system—the move away from defined benefit plans to defined contribution plans and the advent of the healthcare exchanges—it is becoming clearer that consumers can indeed begin to shop meaningfully for the healthcare they need. There is increasing demand for more and more information that consumers can use to be better shoppers, and several companies are working hard to bring these healthcare marketplaces to consumers.

The shift to a defined contribution model makes too much sense for it not to be embraced by a great number of employers in the next few years. The exchanges—public and private—will also fuel this desire in consumers to be able to shop and find the best fit for their individual situations.

The transformative aspect that brings all of this to reality on a wide scale is technology—sophisticated technology—that allows this transformation of our system to occur on a seamless basis. The winners in this transformation will be the companies that can deliver this new system, the employers and ACOs who see the value in these changes, and the healthcare consumer, who gets more value and better outcome.

Free Market Harnessing Economic Outcomes of High Quality

All of this change is going to take time. We believe that the transformative changes will be incremental at first, but that the free market will take hold and propel things forward. The consumer will assume a position of power that he has never before held in the healthcare system.

The advent of the exchanges, and the technology associated with them, are going to enable and engage consumers in a long-term view of both their health benefits and their retirement situations. As the transparency of the data increases, the technology will drive consumer behavior more and more towards the free market. These changes will improve the consumer health experience, enable better planning, improve consumer health decision-making, and improve our long-term quality of life.

A rough couple of decades, in the financing and delivery of healthcare, leads us to expect even greater challenges in the near future. After years of attempts to centralize control over medical decisions and dollars, the next phase will lead us in a direction that will finally reunite patients with their own health, healthcare, and healthcare dollars.

> All of this change is going to take time. We believe that the transformative changes will be incremental at first, but that the free market will take hold and propel things forward.

History shows us how this will likely play out. Extravagant healthcare funding beginning in the mid-1960's led to decades of unrestrained spending and was followed by unsuccessful attempts to contain costs. In the 1990's managed care introduced business concepts that were otherwise foreign to the world of healthcare. The result was a much-needed taming of expenditures, but at the price of denials, delays, and inconveniences that sometimes were medically, personally, politically, and even economically counterproductive. Although healthcare clearly needed business discipline, many of the tools of managed care came from people who had considerable experience with businesses such as insurance, but little experience with the clinical nuances of healthcare.

The belt tightening tactics regarding managed care quickly faded, partly through public backlash and partly as the late 1990's economic boom required employers to lure and retain good workers with generous healthcare benefits alongside hefty salaries. This phase, too, was short-lived as the most recent economic recession now forces another reexamination of the ways in which healthcare is financed and delivered.

Promising changes are coming through "defined contribution" plans that bring patients into closer contact with the costs of their care and thereby into greater control over the content of their care. This development provides an important opportunity to address longstanding shortcomings in the U.S. healthcare system. So how will these defined contribution plans be delivered? Health insurance exchanges are the most likely vehicle.

Health Insurance Exchanges

The US Department of Health and Human Services (HHS) issued proposed regulations on the establishment of the state health insurance exchanges under the new health reform law, the Patient Protection and Affordable Care Act (ACA).

Even though there is federal funding available for the states to establish ACA exchanges, only 17 states have as of this writing taken mandatory steps establishing an exchange. If a state fails to meet the deadline then HHS will operate the exchange within the state. Exchanges are key to the law's goals to expand coverage and lower costs for health insurance. Beginning in 2014, individuals and small businesses (defined below) will be able to purchase health insurance through the exchanges. Exchanges will certify standardized health plans (referred to as qualifying health plans or QHPs) that provide different levels of coverage for "essential health benefits," based on the following actuarial values of coverage of benefits provided under the particular plan:

- Bronze level-60 percent
- Silver level-70 percent
- Gold level-80 percent; and
- Platinum level-90 percent

The law defines "essential health benefits" to include any of the following categories of benefits:

- Outpatient services
- Emergency services
- Hospitalization
- Maternity and newborn care
- Mental health and substance use disorder services
- Behavioral health treatment
- Prescription drugs
- Rehabilitative and habilitative services and devices
- Laboratory services
- Preventive and wellness services
- Chronic disease management
- Pediatric services, including oral and vision care

Beginning in 2014, people without access to affordable, qualifying coverage through their employer may qualify for federal subsidies for coverage purchased through the exchange. The subsidies, which are only available for coverage purchased through the state-operated exchange, include premium tax credits and cost-sharing reductions. However, to qualify, a person's household income must be under four times the federal poverty level (generally $89,400 for a family of four in 2011 dollars).

Timing and Benefits

Exchanges are intended to provide access to affordable coverage for small employers and for individuals who buy their own insurance. The Congressional Budget Office estimates that up to 29 million people will secure private insurance coverage through exchanges when they are fully operational.

When will exchanges be operational?

State exchanges must be up and running by January 2014. However, states must meet numerous requirements for the establishment of their exchanges prior to October 2013, which is the deadline for federal approval of state exchanges. If a state does not meet the federal benchmarks, the federal government will step in and run the exchange or parts of the exchange functions in a partnership with the state.

Who Qualifies for Coverage Through an Exchange?

Individuals and small employers can apply to purchase health coverage through an exchange. It's important to note that the exchange for individual coverage within a state will operate separately from the small employer exchange (small business health options program or SHOP), unless the state merges its individual and small group markets. Insurers can also offer stand-alone, limited scope dental plans through the exchanges.

"Small employer" means an employer of at least one employee on the first day of the plan year, but no more than 100 employees during the preceding calendar year, taking into account all companies within the employer's controlled group (generally, companies related by at least 80 percent common stock ownership). However, prior to 2016, states can choose to define a small employer as an employer that employed no more than 50 employees during the preceding calendar year. By 2015, each state's insurance exchange must be self-supporting and will not receive any additional federal money. Thus, the exchanges will likely apply assessments or user fees on the insurer's participating in the exchange. Beginning in 2017, each state will have the option of opening its SHOP exchange to all employers, regardless of size.

State Exchange

An exchange must be operated by either a state governmental agency or a nonprofit entity established by the state. Health insurers can offer plans within the exchange, but cannot be a sponsor of a state exchange or be a service provider to the exchange. States will need approval from The Department of Health and Human Services ("HHS") to start operating the exchanges. As you would expect, approval requires the ability to demonstrate operational readiness and to provide the following functions:

1. Certifying health plans that qualify for being offered through the exchange. Health insurers must offer at least one silver level and one gold level plan through the exchange, as well as a child-only plan. The health insurer must charge the premium rates without regard to whether the plan is offered through an exchange.

Note: States would have the option of allowing all qualifying health plans to participate or imposing more restrictive rules; for example, using competitive bidding to select plans.

2. Performing eligibility determinations for enrollees, including an appeals process, as well as tracking and reporting terminations of coverage.

3. Enrolling individuals in health plans via a single, streamlined application and transmitting the necessary information to the insurer.

4. Meeting standards for financial stability, oversight, quality, and the protection of confidential information (including enrollees' protected health information and Social Security numbers).

5. Providing a premium tax credit calculator so enrollees can calculate government subsidies.

6. Providing customer assistance tools such as a call center, Internet Web site, and a provider directory.

7. Establishing a "navigator program" that allows potential enrollees to comparison shop for coverage and enroll in plans.

An exchange must be ready to accept enrollees on October 1, 2013. HHS must approve a state's exchange by no later than January 1, 2013, although HHS will grant conditional approvals for states that are moving forward. If a state fails to meet the deadline, then HHS is tasked with operating the exchange within the state.

Two states, Massachusetts and Utah, have exchanges that pre-date federal health reform. The HHS proposed rules indicate that a state health exchange in operation on January 1, 2010, is deemed to qualify under the federal standards only if the state's percentage of insureds is at least the national average after the implementation of the health reform law. The practical impact of this proposed rule is that the Massachusetts exchange (The Connector) would qualify under the federal standards, but the Utah exchange would not.

Although exchanges will operate on a state-by-state basis, the law allows states to band together to offer a regional exchange (although there has been little interest in doing so to date). HHS will also allow subsidiary exchanges within a state that serves a geographically distinct area.

How Will Individuals Enroll in Coverage Through the Exchange?

Many of the enrollment rules that will apply to exchange coverage are similar to rules used by employer health plans. For example, exchanges must provide individuals with an initial open enrollment period, an annual open enrollment period, and a special enrollment period when a person gains a dependent or loses other coverage.

The initial open enrollment period begins October 1, 2013, and extends through February 28, 2014. Coverage will be effective on January 1, 2014, for people who elect coverage on or before December 23, 2013. Otherwise, coverage is generally effective the first day of the month following the individual's election.

Each year, the exchange must offer an annual open enrollment that allows individuals to add coverage or change health plans. The annual open enrollment period will be between October 15th through December 7th of each year, with coverage effective on the following January 1st. For example, the open enrollment period for 2015 will be from October 15, 2014, through December 7, 2014, with coverage being effective January 1, 2015.

Special enrollment periods allow an individual 60 days from a triggering event (certain life events or coverage changes) to enroll or change plans. Coverage is effective on the first day of the following month if the individual elects coverage by the 22nd day of the previous month, subject to a special rule that applies retroactive coverage for birth, adoption, or placement for adoption of a child. The triggering events that allow a special enrollment period are:

1. The individual (or dependent) loses minimum essential coverage, including coverage under an employer plan, for reasons other than failure to pay premiums or situations that allow a rescission of coverage (e.g., fraud).

2. The person gains a dependent or becomes a dependent through marriage, birth, adoption, or placement for adoption.

3. An individual who was not previously a citizen, national, or lawfully present gains this status.

4. The individual's enrollment or non-enrollment in a health plan is unintentional, inadvertent, or erroneous and is the result of the error, misrepresentation, or inaction of an officer, employee, or agent of the exchange or HHS.

5. An enrollee adequately demonstrates to the exchange that the health plan in which he or she is enrolled substantially violated a material provision of its contract in relation to the individual.

6. An individual is determined newly eligible or newly ineligible for the premium tax credit or has a change in eligibility for cost-sharing reductions, regardless of whether such individual is already enrolled in a health plan.

Note: The exchange must permit an individual whose existing coverage through an employer-sponsored plan will no longer be qualifying or affordable for his or her employer's upcoming plan year to access a special enrollment period prior to the end of his or her coverage through such employer-sponsored plan.

7. The individual or enrollee gains access to new health plans as a result of a permanent move.

8. The individual or enrollee meets other "exceptional circumstances" as the exchange or HHS may provide.

The events noted above do not allow the individual to change the level of coverage (e.g., move from a bronze plan to a gold plan), subject to an exception for number six (eligibility for subsidy).

> There won't be instant acceptance from any of the parties in the healthcare system. There is a high, and very definite, uncertainty about how things will ultimately play out. Employers are not necessarily going to want to jump in the pool and get all wet, but they might want to test the water with their toe.

There won't be instant acceptance from any of the parties in the healthcare system. There is a high, and very definite, uncertainty about how things will ultimately play out. Employers are not necessarily going to want to jump in the pool and get all wet, but they might want to test the water with their toe. Several companies offer them the opportunity to begin the transition to a new way of looking at healthcare for their employees. They can help them—and their employees—embrace the concept of the exchange. It's part of the incremental steps that can get them at least part way down the path and perhaps ready for the next step.

There will be considerable discussion in the media and by our federal and state policymakers as the deadline for implementing changes, like the exchanges, gets closer. Deadlines may be delayed or modified. All of the participants in the system need to seek out neutral, agnostic advice to navigate what is ahead. It's not going to be easy.

SECTION V
MAKING CHOICES

This section is about next steps for both employers and individuals: how can both segments align themselves best for what lies ahead?

Choices – Employees and Individuals

Individuals have two relatively straightforward paths that they will need to navigate when the provisions of the Affordable Care Act take effect in 2014. The Act requires virtually all individuals to have health insurance coverage, whether that coverage is provided by an employer or purchased by the individual.

If an individual is currently insured or covered with health insurance by his or her employer, then he or she is set in terms of the coverage mandate. If his or her employer does not offer its employees any health coverage, and the individual is still required to purchase health insurance, then the individual will need to take advantage of the state's public exchange (or private market) in order to satisfy the coverage mandate. If the individual does not purchase health insurance, he is subject to a penalty. In 2014, that penalty is $95, a relatively insignificant amount compared to even the minimum annual health insurance premium. It is likely that penalty will gradually increase each year until it becomes a more significant deterrent.

> If an individual is currently insured or covered with health insurance by his or her employer, then he or she is set in terms of the coverage mandate.

Every individual will have to demonstrate his or her compliance with the insurance coverage mandate. Compliance is met by either paying the $95 penalty (probably on the individual's income tax return), or visiting the public insurance exchange provided in his state to examine available options. And while the minimum benefit set plans on the public exchanges have not yet been established in all cases, regardless of what is ultimately offered, the individual will be able to determine whether he qualifies for a tax credit, or subsidy, or for Medicaid, depending on status and need. Those additional options might make coverage that was once unaffordable, affordable and desirable.

The subsidies and tax credits are expected to be available on a relatively generous basis—they are designed to help the middle class be able to afford healthcare as well as the economically disadvantaged.

If the individual is covered by an employer's plan, the individual should take an active interest in what types of benefits are offered and how he or she can make the best of whatever is offered.

Choices – Employers

The next steps for employers are really based on the answers to several choices that each employer needs to make regarding its future interface with the healthcare system.

Choice #1: Will the company offer health benefits to its employees?

Looking broadly across the board, approximately 61 percent of the corporate universe offers health benefits and 39 percent do not. Some analysts believe that because of the Affordable Care Act, we might see that percentage of employers offering health benefits actually decline, especially at the lower end of the range in terms of number of employees. The expectation by some is that employers with 50 or fewer employees may decide to no longer offer health benefits.

<u>Choice #2</u>: If the company offers health benefits, will they be based on the defined benefit or defined contribution model?

As we covered in previous sections, the defined benefit plans are the way employee benefits have mostly been done in this country for decades. It is a limited, fixed menu of benefits that employees are allowed to choose from. The employer drives the process of creating the menu of available choices through its relationship with an insurer or insurance broker. These plans are reviewed, and the available benefits adjusted annually and recently the trend line is for increasing premiums and decreasing levels of coverage.

The defined contribution model is seen as the wave of the future in employee healthcare benefits because it allows the employer to define a contribution it will make on behalf of the employee for his or her use in choosing benefits from a broader spectrum of plans and coverage. This system is driven more toward predictable costs and employee driven choices, to even include benefits beyond major medical coverage like dental, vision, life, or disability insurance, as well as tax-advantaged plans such as flexible spending arrangements, health reimbursement arrangements, and health savings accounts.

<u>Choice #3</u>: Will the employer supplement the benefit offering with additional tax advantaged plans?

Offering these types of accounts within the defined contribution model can be a significant benefit to both the employer and the employee. The employer benefits by (possibly) reducing his liability for Social Security taxes because the dollars for these accounts go to the employees on a pre-tax basis. So the employer has something of a tax incentive to provide these types of benefits because it returns money to the employer incrementally. Employees benefit in that they can use funds in these tax-advantaged accounts for purposes of alleviating co-payments and other qualified out of pocket expenses that they might incur during the plan year.

The use of these tax-advantage accounts needs to be spread among individuals because they will be increasingly responsible for out of pocket expenses and deductibles and these accounts can offer significant tax savings on those expenses. For the employer, it's in essence, a payroll reduction strategy since the pre-tax funding allows savings on Social Security tax liability.

If the employer decides to contribute along with the employee to the tax-advantaged plan, that makes the tax-advantaged plan that much more attractive for the individual to participate in, and to the extent that employers can incent individuals to participate in those plans, that participation will help lower the overall cost of healthcare to the individual and to the family. It continues to move the system and the individual toward a more accountable model for healthcare, which we believe is the future of our system.

Choice #4: Will the employer offer more benefits than just medical benefits?

This choice is about the breadth of the employer's healthcare offering. Is it only major medical coverage, or is it a benefits offering that includes other coverage like dental, vision, life, or disability insurance? Will there be educational or wellness initiatives involved?

For the employee, the convenience of being able to make all of his healthcare decisions in one place with a broad selection of options is very desirable. Trying to shop the universe of options one by one is most of the time a complete nightmare of apples to oranges comparisons and confusing pricing.

Choice #5: How will the employer deliver the benefits to his employees?

The employer has made his choices. He has chosen to set up a benefits plan. He has chosen the supplemental tax-advantaged plans to offer his employees. He's ready to go. How does he do it?

We believe that the answer going forward will be the deployment of the private exchange model. It's an easy, intuitive way for an employer to then present these possibilities to his employee population in a transparent format that allows true cost comparison. There's no broker or insurance company pushing a particular product—the information and choices are presented in a neutral, agnostic manner. The process (and the administrative aspects going forward) will be electronic, as opposed to paper-based, resulting in greatly increased efficiency. A private exchange makes sense for an employer to set up. Providers can sponsor the private exchange to create an environment where all goes forward in as seamless and efficient a manner as possible with the least amount of employee anxiety.

> We believe that the answer going forward will be the deployment of the private exchange model.

It's also far less of a burden for the employer and it can all be done in a week, as opposed to a month or two.

Business Models

As we head into this new era of more accountable healthcare, we believe that we are also headed into an era of new business models surrounding the provision of that healthcare, both on the part of the healthcare industry and for employers.

> As we head into this new era of more accountable healthcare, we believe that we are also headed into an era of new business models surrounding the provision of that healthcare both on the part of the healthcare industry and for employers.

We see an evolution toward a more consumer-engaged business model, a more consumer-driven business environment. It's a radical change from where we are now. Consumers will be responsible for their own healthcare choices and the industry and employers have to develop much more support to help people make those decisions and choices.

The trend toward consumer-directed healthcare is accelerating and is nearly unstoppable at this point. We're rapidly getting to that point in the healthcare arena where the same types of decisions and control that consumers have around their retirement and investments will now extend to healthcare.

The path ahead is not certain for anyone involved with healthcare. The Affordable Care Act has changed the landscape for all stakeholders and created another area of uncertainty in a world already full of uncertainty. And even though our healthcare system was on a clearly unsustainable path marked by increasing costs and declining benefits,

OVERDOSE: Your Health, My Money

billions of dollars wasted in inefficiency and unnecessary care, it was at least an environment that we were used to.

The new paradigm of healthcare sheds light on a broken system and provides us pathways for employers to take the right incremental steps forward as the fog dissipates and the path ahead becomes clear. We believe there are means for taking those incremental steps that can have a transformative impact on the healthcare system as a whole by fostering the overall goals of the Affordable Care Act and increasing the quality of the delivery of healthcare.

> The new paradigm of healthcare sheds light on a broken system and provides us pathways for employers to take the right incremental steps forward as the fog dissipates and the path ahead becomes clear.

The change is going to be achieved through technology, connectivity, and better and more complete information available to consumers. They can then take advantage of this more transparent environment to make their own revolutionary decisions and begin to transform their own personal health and wellness, which in turn will transform the healthcare system in this country.

We believe that the Affordable Care Act is a starting point. Achieving everything its drafters set out to do is a little like trying to boil the ocean—a little too much to try all at once. There is a tremendous amount of skepticism concerning the Act across the spectrum from the politicians to the consumer. There will be considerable pain felt in offices of middle and upper management in companies, legislative chambers, and living rooms trying to figure out how best to implement the letter and spirit of the Act.

> We believe that the Affordable Care Act is a starting point.

We believe that there is a solution that can relieve some of that pain and integrate the experience, integrate the inter-operability of the exchange, and allow people to have an experience that is educational, that is efficient, and that works in the best interests of employers and their employees.

It's all about being able to navigate your health choices. Everyone wins.

OVERVIEW OF CIELOSTAR
AND ITS OFFERINGS

CieloStar
Navigate Your Health Choices

With the passage and enactment of the federal legislation known as the Affordable Care Act, the landscape for healthcare in this country is on course to undergo some dramatic changes. The next several years will require almost every consumer of healthcare—employers and employees alike—to make drastic changes in not only the way that they provide for their healthcare needs, but also in their basic philosophy surrounding healthcare issues. These consumers need expert guidance to make the right decisions in what will become an even more complicated array of choices. CieloStar is a company perfectly positioned to offer expertise that is unequaled in consumer-directed healthcare.

As a leading healthcare benefit, technology, and administration company, Minnesota-based CieloStar offers directed healthcare plan administration, defined contribution benefit administration, healthcare payment processing, risk transfer, health screening, health coaching, consolidated billing, participant communications, enrollment support, COBRA administration, incoming and outgoing call center services, wellness, private exchanges for employers, consumers, affinity groups, and government.

CieloStar began operations in 1988 as a third-party benefit administration firm, emphasizing the technology side of benefit management and administration. By 2000, the company had developed BenefitReady, a kind of proprietary software that allows online enrollment for purposes of employee benefit administration. In the years since 2000, the company has focused on improving and updating the BenefitReady platform so that it allows an integrated, seamless benefits enrollment and management experience for an employer and/

or employees. The company changed its name from OutsourceOne to CieloStar in September 2012.

The company's services are marketed as five distinct product families: CieloSource, providing backroom administration; BenefitReady, providing benefit administration and enrollment; MyCieloChoice, a consumer portal for managing healthcare products and which are the direct to consumer products, and CieloChoice which provides private insurance exchanges, payment processing and wellness offerings. CieloCare combines all aspects of the private exchange technology, back office administration, and call center support, along with risk transfer and medical claims processing to power the evolving Accountable Care Organization and Cooperative Markets.

A Sea Change: Defined Benefit to Defined Contribution

We're at a very important juncture in this country and the old model of healthcare is changing fast. These changes are being forced by decades of runaway, double-digit inflation in healthcare expenditures in this country. At its core, the changes entail a shift away from what would have been traditionally thought of as a defined benefit model to a defined contribution model.

In many ways it is very similar to the shift that occurred in most retirements plans. These have shifted from the traditional company pension—a defined benefit plan—to a retirement landscape dominated by the 401(k) retirement plan—a defined contribution model.

Here's an example of how that shift works in healthcare: instead of an employer offering a set menu of benefits to employees (medical, dental, vision, etc.), that employer will offer a set dollar contribution for the employee to spend on his healthcare needs. This will result in a great deal more choice for consumers, as well as far more complexity involved in those choices.

All of this is opening up a huge, gaping need for some type of tool—a technology tool—to guide consumers through the coming maze. Such tools have been successfully developed and deployed to help with such revolutionary changes in the banking, financial services, and travel industries. This technology will wrap together and provide the background and decision support for all pieces of the healthcare puzzle: major medical, dental, vision, life, disability, and long-term care insurance. And equally important, the technology would allow for the nearly instant payment processing for this healthcare with the goal of eliminating the extremely inefficient and costly payment model of "provide the service, generate a bill, send the bill, find the customer for payment, and then chase the customer for payment."

The greatest example of this kind of transformation into a more efficient transaction model is the banking industry. Not too long ago the concept of obtaining instant cash out of an ATM machine at a local bank branch was hard to imagine—much less having that access in countries all around the world. Today that's exactly what the banking industry has been able to do. Insert a card with one magnetic strip, anywhere in the world, and out will come currency in the local denomination. No questions and no paper involved, unless you want a receipt.

It's imperative that our healthcare delivery system achieves this kind of efficiency. If it does not, the ever-spiraling, astronomical costs will continue to strangle this country's economic possibilities.

Why is this happening? The healthcare system as we currently know it is so incredibly wasteful and inefficient that it has become untenable and absolutely unsustainable. Imagine this scenario: you are an employer and you are having your annual meeting with the insurance broker you use to supply your benefits package for employees. The broker reports happily, "I've done a great job for you this year—your premiums are only going up 12 percent." You know you can't raise your prices by 12 percent. How are you going to pay for that increase? In the past, the only options you had were to change brokers or possibly downsize the benefits available to employees. Because those defined benefits were priced and purchased externally, employers and employees alike were stuck on a treadmill of increasing costs and decreasing benefits.

The only way to get off that treadmill is to change the system and the rules governing it and, thus, change a defined contribution health and benefit system. The employer determines how much he is willing to contribute for the purposes of providing employee benefits, sets up an account for each employee, and then funds that account. The employee then uses the funds in the account to allocate among his or her specific healthcare needs. Depending on his or her needs, the employee can add additional funding to the account. The funding and appropriate plan information is then loaded on a "smart" health card and is then available for the purposes of obtaining and paying for care at point of service.

Consider these examples: An employer sets up an employee account for $6,000. The employee signs up for a high-deductible major medical plan, a vision plan, a dental plan, and a long-term care plan. After all is said and done, there is $1,000 left in the account. That amount is then placed in any variety of pre-tax benefit arrangements like a health reimbursement account or health savings account, all accessible through the use of the "smart" health card. These funds are then available for the employee to use for qualified expenses like co-pays or prescription drugs. Alternatively, the employee has four children and is planning for the need for orthodontics. That employee wants to allocate more dollars toward the dental portion of their particular equation. The increased dental portion brings the total amount to $8,000. The employee contributes the additional $2,000 to obtain all the coverage needed. Any qualified expenses (co-pays, prescription drugs) would then be the responsibility of the employee.

Like PriceLine.com or Kayak.com for Healthcare

CieloStar brings to the table the tool—the technology—to enable the healthcare consumer to make critical choices in a neutral, comparison friendly format. This tool is like PriceLine.com or Kayak.com, but for healthcare rather than for travel. Priceline.com is an information aggregator for deep discounts on hotels, flights, rental cars, vacations, and cruises; Kayak.com allows a user to compare hundreds of individual travel sites to help plan travel needs. Both allow users to truly find and book their best travel choices from a price and schedule perspective.

Employers bring in CieloStar to provide the technology and "back office" capabilities that enable this rich, consumer-driven experience for employees in terms of healthcare. The consumer interface is the tip of spear—the outward facing piece of a technology that is capitalizing on this important juncture in our healthcare system.

CieloStar's vision for this tool is to also include broad ranging program and pricing data as well as wellness initiatives and educational tools to help build consumer knowledge and ultimately more accountability for individual health. Secure, neutral, agnostic, not aligned with any insurance companies, CieloStar presents the consumer with his or her "healthcare dashboard" where all of the critical decisions and planning can be done. It's a technology package presenting sources of data that can work for companies with two employees or tens of thousands.

So just what would an employee see when he sits down to make his healthcare choices? For purposes of this illustration, let's assume his employer has chosen to move to a defined contribution model and has engaged CieloStar to provide the technological solution.

In the set up phase, the employer would have provided the basic information about his employees. CieloStar would use this to pre-populate the database so that when the employee logs on for the first time, the profile screen is already created. The employee would see information about age, gender, home address, salary—other personnel-related information. As one of its first tasks, the system will ask the employee to do is what is called a "dependent audit." This process is designed to verify any dependents the employee has and their status. One of the reasons for this process is that data shows that many times the information an employer has on an employee's dependents is actually incorrect or out of date. These kinds of errors can lead to dependents being covered by a healthcare plan that they are not eligible for—perhaps they are too old or are covered by a plan elsewhere. This might sound pretty basic, and for most employees, redundant, but verifying dependents can be a serious cost-control measure for employers and employees alike. No sense in paying for coverage that is not necessary.

Once the employee has verified his basic information, then it's on to the medical plan options. In our example, the employer has decided to offer two different BlueCross plans and a Kaiser plan. The choices are arrayed for the employee along with real apples-to-apples comparative data—just like one might find on Priceline.com. And the comparative data and rates are all based on the employee's individual information and situation. This intuitive, comparative look is critical here because in most open enrollment situations, the choices are so confusing and so "apples-to-oranges" that most employees don't take the time to find out which option really suits their situation best. They just choose the plan they had last year and move on—get it over with as fast as they can. But there are real differences between the available plans and those differences can manifest themselves after it's too late to change.

The next step would be choosing from any supplemental benefits offered by this employer. These could include dental, vision, disability, long-term care and life insurance. These optional benefits would have their own information and comparative data, just as the major medical coverage did. Once the supplemental benefits screens have been worked through, it's on to flexible spending plans.

This is where the landscape can get a bit complicated. Many employers today in the interest of reducing premium expenses and also in the interest of creating more accountability on the part of the employee to manage his own health related expenses are opting for high-deductible medical plan options. Some of these plans will qualify for a health savings account (HSA); some plans will qualify for an HSA and a flexible spending account (FSA) or a limited flexible spending account that would be used for dental and vision only. Some employers will opt to use a heath reimbursement arrangement (HRA) to go along with all of this. Managing these options is really important because the employee is able to set aside dollars on a pre-tax basis to fund these various account options. The CieloStar tool helps them make those decisions by offering them contextual options based on either the data reported by the employee (actual doctor's visits) or available actuarial data based on the employee's age and gender to determine what would be the average expectation for healthcare expenses. All of this helps the employee determine just how to allocate funds for these accounts.

This process results in a final review where the employee can see in one snapshot all of their healthcare benefits. Once the employee has finished enrollment, and is using his healthcare benefits, he can come back to the planning tool to monitor his expenses and benefit usage during the year. He can also access wellness-related information and resources from there as well.

So how does the employee "spend" his benefits so that the money for a particular doctor visit or dental procedure is billed to the correct insurance provider or comes out the proper tax advantaged account he set up in his enrollment? The final piece of the CieloStar solution is the benefit debit card.

Here's an example of how the benefit debit card works. An employee is shopping at Target and wants to pick up a prescription at the pharmacy there. The employee goes to the checkout and swipes this smart health card. It knows that the six-pack of Coke Zero and the potato chips don't qualify, but it does recognize the prescription and pays for that item. The employee then pays cash or uses a different card for his other items.

This approach is so different than the current range of online health management tools. While many people already go to their particular health insurance provider's website and they can access wellness tools, keep their personal health records, and compare coverage. Those tools are based on a single provider's available programs and would be like visiting the website for Delta Airlines to find travel options for a trip to New York—the only options presented will be from Delta, not Jet Blue or Virgin. And guess what happens to all that wellness information and personal health records the employee has taken the time to input on the Blue Shield site if he or she decides to go to Kaiser next year? It all disappears.

CieloStar offers a tool that truly raises the bar on consumer-directed healthcare tools. The only path to real choice and understanding all options is an unbiased, neutral resource presenting a far broader, multi-provider landscape of options.

REFERENCES

1. Abraham, K. s. (1981) "Judge-Made Law and Judge-Made Insurance: Honoring the Reasonable Expectations of the Insured." Virginia Law Review 67: 1151-91.

2. American College of Physicians (1996) "Voluntary Purchasing Pools: A Market Model for Improving Access, Quality, and Cost in Healthcare." Annals of Internal Medicine 124: 845-53.

3. Anders, C. (1995) "Once a Host Specialty, Anesthesiology Cools as Insurers Scale Back." Wall Street Journal (17 March): AI.

4. Anders, C. (1996) "Who Pays Cost of Cut-Rate Heart Care?" Wall Street Journal (15 October): B1.

5. Anderson, G.; Hall, M. A.; and Steinberg, E. P. (1993) "Medical Technology Assessment and Practice Guidelines: Their Day in Court." American Journal of Public Health 83: 1635-39.

6. Andrews-Clarke v. Travelers Ins., Co. (1997) 984 F.Supp. 49 (D. Mass.). Azevedo, D. (1995) "New Strategies for Clamping DO'WTI on Referrals." Medical Economics 72(7): 58-73.

7. Barr, D. A. (1995) "The Effects of Organizational Structure on Primary Outcomes under Managed Care." Annals of Internal Medicine 122: 353- 59.

8. Berk, M. L., and Monheit, A. C. (2001) "The Concentration of Healthcare Expenditures, Revisited." Health Affairs 20(2): 9-18.

9. Blumenthal, D. (2001) "Controlling Healthcare Expenditures." New England Journal of Medicine 344: 766--69.

10. Butler, S., and Haislmaier, E. F., eds. (1989) Critical Issues: A National Health System for America. Washington, D.C.: The Heritage Foundation.

11. Delbanco, T. L.: Meyers, K. c.; and Segal, E. A. (1979) "Paying the Physician's Fee: Blue Shield and the Reasonable Charge." New

England Journal of Medicine 301: 1314-20.

12. Dudley, R. A., and Luft, H. A. (2001) "Managed Care in Transition." New England Journal of Medicine 344: 1087-92.

13. Epstein, R. M. (1995) "Communication Between Primary Care Physicians and Consultants." Archives of Family Medicine 4: 403-9.

14. Ferber, J. D. (1996) "Auto-assignment and Enrollment in Medicaid Managed Care Programs." Journal of Law, Medicine & Ethics 24: 99-107.

15. Gerber, P. D.; Smith, D. S.; and Ross, J. M. (1994) "Generalist Physicians and the New Healthcare System." American Journal of Medicine 97: 554-58.

16. Crumbach, K., and Bodenheimer, T. (1995) "The Organization of Healthcare." Journal of the American Medical Association 273: 160-67.

17. Hall, M. A. (1994) "The Ethics of Healthcare Rationing." Public Affairs Quarterly 8(1): 33-50.

18. Havighurst, C. C. (1986) "Private Reform of Tort-Law Dogma: Market Opportunities and Legal Obstacles." Law and Contemporary Problems 49: 143-72.

19. Herdrich v. Pegram (1998) 154 F.3d 362 (7th Cir.).

20. Hilzenrath, D. S. (1995) "Cutting Costs-or Quality?" Washington Post Weekly Edition (28 August-3 September): 6.

21. Hoffman, S. (1999) "A Proposal for Federal Legislation to Address Health Insurance Coverage for Experimental and Investigational Treatments." Oregon Law Review 78(1): 203-74.

22. Johannes, L. (1996) "More HMOs Order Outpatient Mastectomies." Wall Street Journal (6 November): Bl.

23. Johnsson, J. (1997) "New Incentive Rules Offer First Curbs on Capitation." American Medical News (27 January): 3.

24. Kaplan, S. H.; Greenfield, S.; Gandek, B.; Rogers, W. H.; and Ware, J. E., Jr. (1996) "Characteristics of Physicians with Participatory Decision-Making Styles." Annals of Internal Medicine 124: 497-504.

25. Kaplan, S. H.; Greenfield, S.; and Ware, J. E., Jr. (1989) "Assessing the Effects of Physician-Patient Interactions on the Outcomes of Chronic Disease." Medical Care 27(3) supplement: Sl10-27.

26. Kassirer, J. P. (1994) "Access to Specialty Care." New England Journal of Medicine 331: 1151-53.

27. Korobkin, R. (1999) "The Efficiency of Managed Care 'Patient Protection' Laws: Incomplete Contracts, Bounded Rationality, and Market Failure." Cornell Law Review 85: 1-88.

28. Kuttner, R. (1999) "The American Healthcare System: Wall Street and Healthcare." New England Journal of Medicine 340: 664-68.

29. Larson, E. (1996) "The Soul of an HMO." Time 147(4): 44-52.

30. Light, D. W. (1983) "Is Competition Bad?" New England Journal of Medicine 309: 1315-19.

31. Meyer, M., and Murr, A. (1994) "Not My Healthcare." Newsweek 123(2) (10 January): 36-38.

32. Miller, J. E. (2001) "A Perfect Storm: The Confluence of Forces Affecting Healthcare Coverage." Washington, D.C.: National Coalition on Healthcare (November).

33. Morreim, E. H. (1994) "Redefining Quality by Reassigning Responsibility." American Journal of Law and Medicine 20: 79-104.

34. E. Haavi Morreim (1998) "Revenue Streams and Clinical

Discretion." Journal of the American Geriatrics Society 46(3): 331-37.

35. E. Haavi Morreim (2001) Holding Healthcare Accountable: Law and the New Medical Marketplace. New York: Oxford University Press.

36. Ogrod, E. S. (1997) "Compensation and Quality: A Physician's View." Health Affairs 16(3): 82-86.

37. Orentlicher, D. (1996) "Paying Physicians More to Do Less: Financial Incentives to Limit Care." University of Richmond Law Review 30(1): 155- 97.

38. Parrish, M. (2001) "A New Day Dawns ... When Patients Buy Their Own Healthcare." Medical Economics. 78(5): 95-111.

39. Pear, R. (2001) "Budget Office's Estimates for Drug Spending Grow." New York Times (24 February): A7.

40. Robert Pear (2001) "Drug Spending Grows Nearly 19%." New York Times (8 May): AI.

41. Pegram v. Herdrich (2000) 530 U.S. 211

42. Robinson, J. (2001) "The End of Managed Care." Journal of the American Medical Association 285: 2622-28.

43. Robinson, J. C., and Casalino, L. P -. (1996) "Vertical Integration and Organizational Networks in Healthcare." Health Affairs 15(1): 7-22.

44. Roe, B. B. (1981) "The UCR Boondoggle: A Death Knell for Private Practice." New England Journal of Medicine 305: 41-45.

45. Rogers, M.C.; Snyderman, R.; and Rogers, E. L. (1994) "Cultural and Organizational Implications of Academic Managed-Care Networks." New England Journal of Medicine 331:. 1374-77.

46. Roulidis, A. C; and Schulrnan K. A. (1994) "Physician

Communication in Managed Care Organizations: Opinions of Primary Care Physicians." Journal of Family Practice 39: 446-51.

47. Schauffler, H. H.; Brown, C.; and Milstein, A. (1999) "Raising the Bar: The Use of Performance Cuarantees by the Pacific Business Group on Health." Health Affairs 18(2): 134-42.

48. Sederer, L. 1. (1994) "Managed Mental Healthcare and Professional Compensation." Behavioral Sciences and the Law 12: 367-78.

49. Shea, S.; Misra, D.; Ehrlich, M. H.; Field, L.; and Francis, C. H. (1992) "Predisposing Factors for Severe, Uncontrolled Hypertension in an InnerCity Minority Population." New England Journal of Medicine 327: 776-81.

50. Starr, P. (1982) The Social Transformation of American Medicine. New York: Basic Books.

51. Sulmasy, D. P. (1995) "Managed Care and Managed Death." Archives of Internal Medicine 155: 133-36.

52. Terry, K. (2001) "Has Capitation Reached Its High-Water Mark?" Medical Economics 78(4): 33-42.

53. Thurow, L. c. (1984) "Learning to Say 'No'." New England Journal of Medicine 311: 1569-72.

54. Shattuck Lecture (1985) "Medicine Versus Economics." New England Journal of Medicine 313: 611-14.

55. Twedt, S. (1996) "Ill-Trained Aides Doing Nurse Work." Memphis Commercial Appeal (25 February): A7.

56. Wall Street Journal (2001) "The Cost Fever Returns." 21 February: R3 (citing sources: William M. Mercer Inc., Milliman & Robertson Inc., Health Affairs, Census Bureau).

57. Winslow, R., and McGinley, L. (2001) "Back on the Front Burner." Wall Street Journal (21 February): R3.

58. Woolhandler, S., and Himmelstein, D. U. (1995) "Extreme Risk-The New Corporate Proposition for Physicians." New England Journal of Medicine 333: 1706-8.

59. Wye River Group on Healthcare et al. (2001) An Employer's Guide to Consumer-Directed Healthcare Benefits. (www.ncpa. org/extra/health/ wye_full.pdf.)

60. Zimmerman, R. (2000) "Drug Spending Soared 17.4% During 1999," Wall Street Journal (27 June): A

GLOSSARY

HIPAA: The Health Insurance Portability and Accountability Act of 1996 (HIPAA; Pub.L. 104–191, 110 Stat. 1936, enacted August 21, 1996) was enacted by the United States Congress and signed by President Bill Clinton in 1996.

PPACA: The Patient Protection and Affordable Care Act (PPACA), commonly called Obamacare or the federal healthcare law, or, for short, Affordable Care Act ("ACA"), is a United States federal statute signed into law by President Barack Obama on March 23, 2010.

Guaranteed Issue
Guaranteed issue will require policies to be issued regardless of any medical condition, and partial community rating will require insurers to offer the same premium to all applicants of the same age and geographical location without regard to gender or most pre-existing conditions (excluding tobacco use).

Health Insurance Exchange: Health insurance exchanges will commence operation in each state, offering a marketplace where individuals and small businesses can compare policies and premiums, and buy insurance (with a government subsidy if eligible).

ACO: An accountable care organization (ACO) is a healthcare organization characterized by a payment and care delivery model that seeks to tie provider reimbursements to quality metrics and reductions in the total cost of care for an assigned population of patients. A group of coordinated healthcare providers forms an ACO, which then provides care to a group of patients. The ACO may use a range of payment models (capitation, fee-for-service with asymmetric or symmetric shared savings, etc.). The ACO is accountable to the patients and the third-party payer for the quality, appropriateness and efficiency of the healthcare provided. According to the Centers for Medicare and

Medicaid Services (CMS), an ACO is "an organization of healthcare providers that agrees to be accountable for the quality, cost, and overall care of Medicare beneficiaries who are enrolled in the traditional fee-for-service program who are assigned to it.

FSA: A flexible spending account (FSA), also known as a flexible spending arrangement, is one of a number of tax-advantaged financial accounts that can be set up through a cafeteria plan of an employer in the United States. An FSA allows an employee to set aside a portion of earnings to pay for qualified expenses as established in the cafeteria plan, most commonly for medical expenses but often for dependent care or other expenses. Money deducted from an employee's pay into an FSA is not subject to payroll taxes, resulting in substantial payroll tax savings. One significant disadvantage to using an FSA is that funds not used by the end of the plan year are lost to the employee, known as the "use it or lose it" rule.

CDH: Consumer-driven healthcare (CDHC), defined narrowly, refers to third tier health insurance plans that allow members to use health savings accounts (HSAs), Health Reimbursement Accounts (HRAs), or similar medical payment products to pay routine healthcare expenses directly, while a high-deductible health plan (HDHP) protects them from catastrophic medical expenses. High-deductible policies cost less, but the user pays routine medical claims using a pre-funded spending account, often with a special debit card provided by a bank or insurance plan. If the balance on this account runs out, the user then pays claims just like under a regular deductible. Users keep any unused balance or "rollover" at the end of the year to increase future balances, or to invest for future expenses.

HRA: Health Reimbursement Accounts or Health Reimbursement Arrangements (HRAs) are Internal Revenue Service (IRS)-sanctioned employer-funded, tax advantaged employer health benefit plan that reimburses employees for out of pocket medical expenses and individual health insurance premiums. Using a Health Reimbursement Account yields "tax advantages to offset healthcare costs" for both employees as well as employers.

HSA: A health savings account (HSA) is a tax-advantaged medical savings account available to taxpayers in the United States who are enrolled in a high-deductible health plan (HDHP).The funds contributed to an account are not subject to federal income tax at the time of deposit. Unlike a flexible spending account (FSA), funds roll over and accumulate year to year if not spent. HSAs are owned by the individual, which differentiates them from company-owned

MCO: The term managed care or managed healthcare is used in the United States to describe a variety of techniques intended to reduce the cost of providing health benefits and improve the quality of care ("managed care techniques") for organizations that use those techniques or provide them as services to other organizations ("managed care organization" or "MCO"), or to describe systems of financing and delivering healthcare to enrollees organized around managed care techniques and concepts ("managed care delivery systems").

PPO: In health insurance in the United States, a preferred provider organization (or PPO, sometimes referred to as a participating provider organization or preferred provider option) is a managed care organization of medical doctors, hospitals, and other healthcare providers who have covenanted with an insurer or a third-party administrator to provide healthcare at reduced rates to the insurer's or administrator's clients.

ICD-10: ICD-10 is the 10th revision of the International Statistical Classification of Diseases and Related Health Problems (ICD), a medical classification list by the World Health Organization (WHO). It codes for diseases, signs and symptoms, abnormal findings, complaints, social circumstances, and external causes of injury or diseases.

The code set allows more than 14,400 different codes and permits the tracking of many new diagnoses. The codes can be expanded to over 16,000 codes by using optional sub-classifications. The detail reported by ICD can be further increased, with a simplified multi-axial approach, by using codes meant to be reported in a separate data field.

The WHO provides detailed information about ICD online, and makes available a set of materials online, such as an ICD-10 online browser,ICD-10 Training, ICD-10 online training, ICD-10 online training support,and study guide materials for download.

The International version of ICD should not be confused with national Clinical Modifications of ICD that frequently include much more detail, and sometimes have separate sections for procedures. The US ICD-10 CM, for instance, has some 68,000 codes. The US also has ICD-10 PCS, a procedure code system not used by other countries that contains 76,000 codes. Work on ICD-10 began in 1983 and was completed in 1992.

ACH: Automated Clearing House (ACH) is an electronic network for financial transactions in the United States. ACH processes large volumes of credit and debit transactions in batches. ACH credit transfers include direct deposit payroll and vendor payments. ACH direct debit transfers include consumer payments on insurance premiums, mortgage loans, and other kinds of bills. Debit transfers also include new applications such as the point-of-purchase (POP) check conversion pilot program sponsored by NACHA – The Electronic Payments Association. Both the government and the commercial sectors use ACH payments. Businesses increasingly use ACH online to have customers pay, rather than via credit or debit cards.

Rules and regulations that govern the ACH network are established by NACHA (formerly the National Automated Clearing House Association) and the Federal Reserve. In 2011, this network processed an estimated 20.2 billion ACH transactions with a total value of $33.91 trillion. Credit card payments are handled by separate networks.

The Federal Reserve Banks are collectively the nation's largest automated clearing house operator, and in 2005 processed 60% of commercial interbank ACH transactions. The Electronic Payments Network (EPN), the only private-sector ACH operator in the U.S., processed the remaining 40%. FedACH is the Federal Reserve's centralized application software used to process ACH transactions. EPN and the Reserve Banks rely on each other for the processing of some transactions when either party to the transaction is not their customer. These interoperator transactions are settled by the Reserve Banks.

Capitation: Capitation is a payment arrangement for healthcare service providers such as physicians or nurse practitioners. It pays a physician or group of physicians a set amount for each enrolled person assigned to them, per period of time, whether or not that person seeks care. These providers generally are contracted with a type of health maintenance organization (HMO) known as an independent practice association (IPA), which enlists the providers to care for HMO-enrolled patients. The amount of remuneration is based on the average expected healthcare utilization of that patient, with greater payment for patients with significant medical history. Rates are also affected by age, race, sex, type of employment, and geographical location, as these factors typically influence the cost of providing care.

PHR: A personal health record, or PHR, is a health record where health data and information related to the care of a patient is maintained by the patient. This stands in contrast with the more widely used electronic medical record, which is operated by institutions (such as a hospital) and contains data entered by clinicians or billing data to support insurance claims. The intention of a PHR is to provide a complete and accurate summary of an individual's medical history which is accessible online. The health data on a PHR might include patient-reported outcome data, lab results, data from devices such as wireless electronic weighing scales or collected passively from a smartphone.

EMR: An electronic medical record (EMR) is a computerized medical record created in an organization that delivers care, such as a hospital or physician's office. Electronic medical records tend to be a part of a local stand-alone health information system that allows storage, retrieval and modification of records.

Health Insurance: Health insurance is insurance against the risk of incurring medical expenses among individuals. By estimating the overall risk of healthcare and health system expenses among a targeted group, an insurer can develop a routine finance structure, such as a monthly premium or payroll tax, to ensure that money is available to pay for the healthcare benefits specified in the insurance agreement. The benefit is administered by a central organization such as a government agency, private business, or not-for-profit entity.

Health Risk Assessment: A health risk assessment (also referred to as a health risk appraisal and health & well-being assessment) is one of the most widely used screening tools in the field of health promotion and is often the first step in multi-component health promotion programs.

A health risk assessment (HRA) is a health questionnaire, used to provide individuals with an evaluation of their health risks and quality of life. Commonly a HRA incorporates three key elements – an extended questionnaire, a risk calculation or score, and some form of feedback, i.e. face-to-face with a health advisor or an automatic online report.

The Centers for Disease Control and Prevention define a HRA as: "a systematic approach to collecting information from individuals that identifies risk factors, provides individualised feedback, and links the person with at least one intervention to promote health, sustain function and/or prevent disease."

There are a range of different HRAs available, however most capture information relating to:
- Demographic characteristics – age, sex
- Lifestyle – exercise, smoking, alcohol intake, diet
- Personal and family medical history (in the US, due to the current interpretation of the Genetic Information Non-discrimination Act, questions regarding family medical history are not permitted if there is any incentive attached to taking a HRA)
- Physiological data – weight, height, blood pressure, cholesterol
- Attitudes and willingness to change behaviour in order to improve health

The main objectives of a HRA are to:

- Assess health status
- Estimate the level of health risk
- Inform and provide feedback to participants to motivate behaviour change to reduce health risks